UNFOLDED

THE STORY OF GOD

D1402604

ERIC GEIGER

LIFEWAY PRESS® NASHVILLE, TENNESSEE

ISBN: 9781462777587
Item Number: 005799068

Dewey Decimal Classification Number: 248.83
Subject Heading:
RELIGION \ CHRISTIAN MINISTRY \ YOUTH

Scripture quotations marked CSB have been taken from the
Christian Standard Bible®, Copyright © 2017 by Holman Bible
Publishers. Used by permission. Christian Standard Bible®
and CSB® are federally registered trademarks of Holman
Bible Publishers.

To order additional copies of this resource, write LifeWay Church
Resources Customer Service; One LifeWay Plaza; Nashville,
TN 37234-0113; FAX order to 615.251.5933; call toll-free
800.458.2772; email orderentry@lifeway.com; order online at
www.lifeway.com; or visit the LifeWay Christian Store serving you.

Printed in the United States of America.

Student Ministry Publishing, LifeWay Church Resources,
One LifeWay Plaza, Nashville, TN 37234

CONTENTS

ABOUT THE
AUTHOR

ERIC GEIGER serves as a Senior Vice President at LifeWay Christian Resources, leading the Resources Division. Eric received his doctorate in leadership and church ministry from Southern Seminary. Eric has authored or co-authored several books including *Creature of the Word* and the best-selling church leadership book, *Simple Church*.

Eric is married to Kaye, and they have two daughters: Eden and Evie. During his free time, Eric enjoys dating his wife, playing with his daughters, and shooting basketball.

INTRODUCTION

Tell me about yourself.

Whether it's on a job interview, a first date, or the first day of school, we've all been asked: Tell me about yourself. It's what we say when we want to get to know someone— to learn about who they really are beyond their basic biographical facts. That's why when someone asks, you don't respond with, "Well, I'm 6-foot-1 and 180 pounds. I was born at 11:43 am on October 3, and my mother's maiden name is Albright." That would be super awkward, and it would totally miss the point. When we ask people to tell us about themselves, we don't want stats—we want a story.

We want to know who they are. What they're passionate about. We want to know what makes them who they really are.

God wants to be known. He is not a silent God. He wants to be known by you. Thankfully, He gave us a Story, in which He reveals Himself fully to us. That's the Bible.

And there's no better story ever written.

We love stories because they're epic. We binge watch season after season, hour after hour, because every season—every series as a whole—tells a story. Each episode is always part of a bigger narrative.

You could watch an episode of *The Office* or *Stranger Things* and get the gist. But if someone pressed you to tell the whole story, you'd have no idea. You wouldn't know how what you saw played into the larger narrative. Knowing the details from one episode is very different from knowing the storyline.

That's how many of us are with the Bible—even those of us who know the stories and have memorized the verses.

Because the Bible is God's story where He reveals Himself to us, we must see it as one story. And there is no better hero, no higher stakes, no greater rescue, and no better ending than what we discover in His story. Every other story pales in comparison. And all of it is true and has deep implications for us today.

That's what is so exciting about the Bible—and why He has invited us in.

HOW TO
USE

Welcome to *Unfolded: The Story of God*. This study is designed to be used in a small group setting with weekly group meetings. However, it could also be used by an individual, in one-on-one mentoring, or adapted for an extended youth retreat.

BIBLE STUDY BOOK

Listed below are the different elements in the Bible study book.

Group Discussion
Questions are provided to help start the conversation.

Personal Study
Four days of personal Bible study will help reinforce the teaching and provide an opportunity to study passages or themes not covered in the group discussion.

Leader Guide
The leader guide at the back of the study provides ideas for activities and deeper discussions.

SESSION OUTLINE

Design your group sessions to fit the space, time, and needs of your guys. The following is a sample group session outline that you can adapt.

1. Opening.
Review the material in the previous week's personal Bible study.

2. Group Discussion.
Scripture and discussion questions are provided to help foster conversation among the group.

3. Closing.
Close the session with prayer.

LEADER
TIPS

Listed below are some tips to make this an effective and meaningful study for you and the young men you lead.

Pray diligently.
Ask God to prepare you to lead this study. Pray individually and specifically for the guys in your group. Make this a priority in your personal walk and preparation.

Prepare adequately.
Don't just wing this. Take time to preview each session so you have a good grasp of the content. Look over the group discussion questions and consider your group of guys. Feel free to delete or reword the questions provided, and add other questions that fit your group.

Provide resources.
Each student will need a Bible study book. Try to have extras on hand for guys who join the group later in the study.

Encourage freely.
Champion the students doing this study, encouraging them to participate in every part of the study.

Lead by example.
Make sure you complete all the personal Bible studies. Be willing to share your story, what you're learning, and your questions as you discuss together.

Be aware.
If guys are hesitant to discuss their thoughts and questions in a larger group, consider dividing into smaller groups to provide a setting more conducive to conversation.

Follow up.
If a participant mentions a prayer request or need, make sure to follow up. It may be a situation where you can get others in the group involved in helping out.

Evaluate often.
After each session and throughout the study, assess what needs to be changed to more effectively lead the study.

THE STORY OF GOD
TIMELINE

2000 BC　　　**1400 BC**　　　**1000 BC**

CREATION & FALL	PROMISE & A PEOPLE	RESCUE & LAW	LAND & KINGDOM

The self-sufficient and eternal God lovingly creates a perfect creation with humanity as His crowning work. Falling for Satan's temptation, humanity rebels, and sin enters the world bringing death, pain, and strife. Instead of giving up on humanity, God promises that from the womb of a woman will come the One who will crush Satan's head.

God pursues Abraham, a man from an idol-worshiping family who has no children with his wife, and promises that he will be the father of many nations. God promises land to Abraham and assures him that all nations will be blessed through his offspring. God continues to be faithful to this family. He restates the promise to Abraham's son Isaac and grandson Jacob (who is renamed Israel). A famine strikes the promised land, so Jacob and the family move to Egypt where one of Jacob's sons, Joseph, is already there to provide for the family.

The family becomes a nation while living in Egypt, but also becomes enslaved to the Egyptians. God raises up Moses to lead His people to freedom. During a tenth plague, God strikes dead the firstborn son of everyone living in Egypt, but "passes over" Israel as they put the blood of lambs on their doorposts. After miraculously rescuing His people, God gives His people the law. He also instructs them to build a tabernacle and offer sacrifices so He may dwell among them.

God brings His people, through their leader Joshua, into the promised land. When God's people worship the gods of the nations surrounding them, God disciplines them through the attacks of surrounding nations. God raises up judges (or rulers) to rescue His people and call them to repentance. They beg for a king to be like other nations, and God gives them Saul. God raises up a new king, David, and promises that his kingdom will never end. The family that turned into a nation is now a kingdom. David's son, Solomon, builds a temple to replace the tabernacle.

600 BC	**AD**	**AD 30**	
	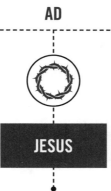		
EXILE & RETURN	**JESUS**	**A NEW PEOPLE**	**A BETTER BEGINNING**

Solomon takes foreign wives and allows their foreign gods to clutter the land. His son continues the line of rulers and the kingdom is divided into the Northern Kingdom (Israel) and the Southern Kingdom (Judah). Prophets confront the people but they persist in their idolatry. The Northern Kingdom falls to Assyria and the Southern Kingdom is carried away into Babylonian captivity. When they are freed, they return to a nation and kingdom far less glorious than before and are still unable to keep their promises.

A descendant of Adam, Abraham, and David, Jesus is the One who crushes the head of Satan, will bless all nations, and reigns forever. Jesus, the God-Man, enters humanity through the womb of a virgin, perfectly obeys the law that we could never obey, dies as the once-and-for-all sacrifice for our sins, and rises from the dead, conquering Satan, sin, and death. He inaugurates His eternal kingdom and secures salvation for His people.

After His ascension to heaven, Jesus sends the promised Holy Spirit and His disciples turn the world upside down preaching the good news of Jesus. In the midst of intense persecution, the gospel spreads, and Gentiles and Jews form a new people. Churches are planted in cities, and apostles write letters encouraging and instructing the people in the grace of Christ and their response to His grace.

A time is coming where God's people—people from every tribe, tongue, and nation who have been rescued by Christ—will enjoy Him and His rule forever in perfect harmony. Satan will be crushed, the effects of sin will be reversed, and all things will be made new.

1

SEASON 1

CREATION & FALL

GOD THE CREATOR AND
CLOTHING MAKER

CREATION & FALL	PROMISE & A PEOPLE	RESCUE & LAW	LAND & KINGDOM	EXILE & RETURN	JESUS	A NEW PEOPLE	A BETTER BEGINNING
	2000 BC	1400 BC	1000 BC	600 BC	AD	AD 30	

WHO IS GOD?

Read Genesis 1:1-5.

Read Genesis 2:4.

From the very beginning, God wants us to know all about who He is. Here are five thoughts to keep in mind about God as He is introducing Himself to us:

1. He **is.**
2. He is the **creator.**
3. He is **self-sufficient.**
4. He is **gracious** and **loving.**
5. He is **powerful** and **wise.**

Which of the five statements about God means the most to you? Why?

WHO ARE WE?

Read Genesis 1:26-27.

You are the crowning work of God's creation. We are not like God, but we are also not like the rest of His creation. Here are three things God intended man to do:

- We were created to **reflect** His image.
- We were created to **rule** over creation.
- We were created to **relate** to others.

What does it mean to reflect God's image as a man?

Why did God think it was important for man to not be alone?

THE MESS WE MADE

Read Genesis 3:1-8.

God was good and gracious by creating us in His image, but we chose to decide for ourselves what was right and wrong. Instead of reflecting His image, we rebelled. Instead of ruling over creation, creation ruled over us.

When was a time you decided for yourself what was right or wrong for your life? What happened?

How does Satan still use the same type of temptation he used in the garden in our lives today?

Why is it significant that Adam and Eve felt shame after they sinned?

OUR HOPE

Read Genesis 3:15 out loud.

This is the first time the gospel is announced—right here in Genesis 3. After God sees us sin, He tells Satan: *A time is coming when there will be One greater than you, who will destroy you.* He's talking about Jesus. Even at the start, the whole epic story of the Bible is pointing to Christ.

Read Genesis 3:21.

Even though Adam and Eve wanted to be in charge, God didn't let them go. Like before, this image points us to Christ and His sacrifice on the cross for our sin: Even as we've rebelled, God pursues us to clothe us with His forgiveness and righteousness.

Why does the gospel show up so early in the story?

In what ways has God pursued you?

SEASON 1

PERSONAL BIBLE STUDY

In our first group session, we discussed
how God introduced Himself by
revealing that He is the One who created
everything—including us. However,
instead of being grateful for His gift of
creation, we, humanity, rebelled against
the rule of God, as seen in Genesis 3.
Our next group session will begin in
Genesis 12, as we focus on God's pursuit
of a people for Himself, through a man
named Abram. The personal studies this
week focus on events that happen in
God's story between the fall of humanity
and the call of Abram.

BROKENNESS & BLESSED EXCHANGE

GENESIS 3:8-19

In the beginning of God's story, we saw Him lovingly create humanity. We were the crowning work of His creation, and everything was perfect. The second chapter in Genesis ends with a statement of peace:

> *This is why a man leaves his father and mother and bonds with his wife, and they become one flesh. Both the man and his wife were naked, yet felt no shame.*
> **GENESIS 2:24-25**

No shame. Can you imagine life with no shame?

No guilt when you make a mistake. No regrets when you wish you had made a different choice. No grief over words you didn't say. Absolutely no shame.

Of course, all that changed in the very next chapter of Genesis when humanity rejected God's rule. Sin entered the world and shame came along with it. Peace was broken. The entrance of sin into the world was not a minor adjustment to God's creation. It affected everything.

Read Genesis 3:8-19 to see the aftermath.

> Look up the word shame in the dictionary and write out the definition below. What did it mean for Adam and Eve to not feel shame? How did their relationship change once they did?

Peace with God was broken.

> *They hid themselves from the LORD God among the trees of the garden.*
> **GENESIS 3:8**

Adam and Eve realized they were naked and hid from the Lord among the trees. Instead of running to God, they ran from him. The "no shame" in Genesis 2 was traded for shame, guilt, and remorse.

Peace with each other was broken.

> *Your desire will be for your husband, yet he will rule over you.*
> **GENESIS 3:16B**

Instead of caring for his wife, Adam turned on her. Like a little kid pointing the finger at his brother, Adam defended himself before God by blaming Eve. This is not the type of men God created us to be—shirking responsibility and shifting blame.

As a consequence of her sin, God told Eve that there would be relational tension between her and her husband. But this doesn't just happen in marriages. All types of relationships have tension now: broken friendships, conflicts with parents and teachers, heated arguments with coaches—all are examples of broken peace.

Peace within ourselves was broken.

> *You will eat from it by means of painful labor all the days of your life.*
> **GENESIS 3:17C**

God told Adam that work would now be filled with painful labor. As a man, all the jobs you hold now and in the future—even if they are awesome and you love what you do—will not ultimately satisfy you. Our souls can only be quenched by God.

What do you see yourself doing in 10 years? Do you think you'll be satisfied?

Peace with our world was broken.

> *The ground is cursed because of you …*
> **GENESIS 3:17B**

Because of the fall, all of creation bears the weight of corruption. Sin has ravaged our world, and we all face the ramifications every day. War, disease, natural disasters, and death are all the results of living in a broken world.

Is there any solution for our brokenness? For the shame we now face?

What are some examples of the brokenness from the fall that you can see in the world?

Thankfully we can read about the shame of Genesis 3 with our eyes fixed on Jesus. When the apostle Paul wrote about marriage several thousand years later, he referenced Genesis 2 to show us how Christ loves us. He wrote:

> *For this reason a man will leave his father and mother and be joined to his wife, and the two will become one flesh. This mystery is profound, but I am talking about Christ and the church.*
> **EPHESIANS 5:31-32**

The word *mystery* here does not refer to something too deep or complex to understand, but to something that was hidden in the Old Testament that has now been revealed for our understanding and enjoyment. And Paul made the mystery clear: "I am talking about Christ and the church." When one becomes a Christian, one is united with Christ.

When Adam and Eve were first united, they felt no shame. When we are united with Christ in faith, there is no shame. Martin Luther called this the Blessed Exchange:

"Faith unites the soul with Christ as a spouse with her husband. Everything which Christ has becomes the property of the believing soul; everything which the soul has becomes the property of the Christ. Christ possesses all blessings and eternal life: they are thenceforward the property of the soul. The soul has all the iniquities and sins: they become thenceforward the property of Christ. It is then a blessed exchange commences."[1]

Read back over this quote again. What does Luther say is being exchanged?

How has Christ turned hopelessness into hope in your life?

DAY 2

- -

MORE STRIFE, BETTER BLOOD

GENESIS 4:1-16

- -

One of the devastating results of sin entering the world is relational conflict, evidenced by hatred and even violence toward one another. We've all been there. We have fought with our parents, our friends, our coaches, and our teachers. Anger has festered in our hearts and bitterness has robbed us of our joy. Even as kids, we fought on playgrounds and sucker-punched kids we didn't like. We can be ruthless. All this began in the garden of Eden.

If only sin had stopped in the garden. But it didn't. It escalated. That's how it always works, apart from God's grace. We see this clearly just one generation after Adam and Eve's devastating choice. Their children demonstrated the devastating and natural progression of sin.

Read Genesis 4:1-16.

Cain was furious because the Lord looked with favor on Abel's offering and not on his. So despite the Lord's warning about being mastered by sin (v. 7), Cain killed his own brother.

When was the last time you let your anger take control? Rate it on a scale of 1–10, then summarize what happened in a few sentences.

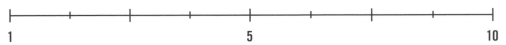

1   5   10

Why did God not receive Cain's offering? What is really going on here? Some verses in the New Testament cast more light on the two brothers.

By faith Abel offered to God a better sacrifice than Cain did. By faith he was approved as a righteous man, because God approved his gifts, and even though he is dead, he still speaks through his faith.
HEBREWS 11:4

For this is the message you have heard from the beginning: We should love one another, unlike Cain, who was of the evil one and murdered his brother. And why did he murder him? Because his works were evil, and his brother's were righteous.
1 JOHN 3:11-12

God receiving Abel's offering and rejecting Cain's was not based on what they offered with their hands, but on the condition of their hearts. Abel offered in faith. Cain's heart was evil, and he proved his evil by killing his brother.

Is that what the world today is really like? Are things really that broken here? Genesis 4 shows us that, indeed, things are not as they were designed to be. The first son born into this world was a murderer.

Then he said, "What have you done? Your brother's blood cries out to me from the ground! So now you are cursed, alienated from the ground that opened its mouth to receive your brother's blood you have shed."
GENESIS 4:10-11

Conflict can poison our relationships. Is there a relationship in your life that's struggling under the weight of conflict? Maybe it's a coach or teacher; maybe it's a girlfriend. Fill in the blanks in these sentences:

My relationship with _____ has too much conflict.

To make things better, I can _____ and _____.

But I also need them to _____.

God, help me to _____.

Cain's sinful rage caused him to spill the blood of his brother, and that blood condemned him. But by God's grace, we have a rescue from this sin, from this hatred. The New Testament tells us that the blood of Jesus speaks a better word—a different word—than the blood of Abel.

...and to Jesus, the mediator of a new covenant, and to the sprinkled blood, which says better things than the blood of Abel.
HEBREWS 12:24

Both Jesus and Abel were innocent and killed by sinful and hateful men. But their spilled blood speaks different messages. The blood of Abel spoke against Cain; the blood of Christ speaks for us. The blood of Abel condemned Cain; the blood of Jesus forgives and justifies us.

We have been like Cain. We have hated, been angry, acted cruelly, and held bitterness and jealously in our hearts. Thankfully, Jesus' blood speaks a better word.

We are not condemned. As Jesus' blood fell to the ground, our liberation and salvation were secured. We are not sent to wander the land, but are welcomed to Him.

Every guy gets angry. But if you let your anger take control, your witness for Christ—and your relationships—will suffer. If you've not repented for your anger, take time now to do so. Then, thank God that the blood of Christ has rescued us from condemnation for our sins.

DAY 3

COSMIC REBOOT

GENESIS 6–9

The space allocated in the Bible to the account of Noah (four chapters) indicates it is a significant event in the story God is telling. When you read the first six chapters of Genesis, you may think, *Wow, that escalated quickly.* In Genesis 2, everything is perfect. God had created everything, declared it to be good, and told Adam and Eve to multiply and steward creation. They enjoyed God and each other in perfect harmony. There was no shame, no sin, no pain, and no death.

Then Adam and Eve rebelled, and their cosmic rebellion had an impact on everything. We still feel the effects today. Adam represents all of us, for all of us have sinned. The image of God is still in us, but it is distorted.

> **Look up some synonyms for the word *distorted*. What does it mean for the image of God to be distorted in us?**

Following the sin of Cain, who murdered his brother, sin spread rampantly. And already by Genesis 6, God had had enough.

> *When the LORD saw that human wickedness was widespread on the earth and that every inclination of the human mind was nothing but evil all the time, the LORD regretted that he had made man on the earth, and he was deeply grieved. Then the LORD said, "I will wipe mankind, whom I created, off the face of the earth, together with the animals, creatures that crawl, and birds of the sky—for I regret that I made them." Noah, however, found favor in the sight of the LORD.*
> **GENESIS 6:5-8**

Noah was not a perfect man, but God expressed grace to him and his family. Noah did not earn God's favor, but rather God graciously gave it to him. You likely know the story: God told Noah to build a massive ark out of wood, so he and his family could be saved from the floodwaters that would destroy the whole earth. Noah and his family took pairs of animals and birds on the ark with them so that life would continue once the flood was over (Gen. 7:1-10).

The flood was absolutely devastating. Read the passage below, circling all the living things the Scripture says were destroyed by the flood.

> *The mountains were covered as the waters surged above them more than twenty feet. Every creature perished—those that crawl on the earth, birds, livestock, wildlife, and those that swarm on the earth, as well as all mankind. Everything with the breath of the spirit of life in its nostrils—everything on dry land died. He wiped out every living thing that was on the face of the earth, from mankind to livestock, to creatures that crawl, to the birds of the sky, and they were wiped off the earth. Only Noah was left, and those that were with him in the ark.*
> **GENESIS 7:20-23**

Sin violates God's holy character and must be punished, yet God is also loving and gracious. So to both punish sin and pardon people, God poured out His wrath through a flood while simultaneously using Noah and an ark to rescue people.

How do we see the picture of Christ illustrated in this story?

Centuries later Jesus came to be our pardon. Just as Noah saved his entire family from the just wrath of God, Jesus saved His family—those who believe in Him—from the punishment for sin.

After Noah and his family were saved and left the ark, Noah built an altar and offered sacrifices to God.

> *Then Noah built an altar to the LORD. He took some of every kind of clean animal and every kind of clean bird and offered burnt offerings on the altar. When the LORD smelled the pleasing aroma, He said to Himself, "I will never again curse the ground because of human beings, even though the inclination of the human heart is evil from his youth onward. And I will never again strike down every living thing as I have done."*
> **GENESIS 8:20-22**

God made a covenant with Noah and promised to never flood the whole earth again. This is the first time we see covenant used in God's story. A covenant is an agreement backed with a promise.

"But you, be fruitful and multiply; spread out over the earth and multiply on it." Then God said to Noah and his sons with him, "Understand that I am establishing my covenant with you and your descendants after you, and with every living creature that is with you—birds, livestock, and all wildlife of the earth that are with you—all the animals of the earth that came out of the ark. I establish my covenant with you that never again will every creature be wiped out by floodwaters; there will never again be a flood to destroy the earth." And God said, "This is the sign of the covenant I am making between me and you and every living creature with you, a covenant for all future generations: I have placed my bow in the clouds, and it will be a sign of the covenant between me and the earth."
GENESIS 9:7-13

Though hurricanes, tsunamis, and other disastrous effects of a fallen and broken world will still strike, the whole earth will never be flooded again. Every time we see a rainbow, we can remember that we have a God who keeps His promises.

As you close today, reread Genesis 9:7 and notice the command God gave Noah. God restated the command "Be fruitful and multiply," which He first gave to Adam and Eve in the garden (Gen. 1:28). God flooded the earth because of our sin, but He did not give up on humanity. He gave them a new start and continued to pursue them. Just as He continues to pursue us. Just as He continues to pursue you.

What evidence in your life shows that God has not given up on you?

GOOD THINGS FOR THE WRONG REASONS

GENESIS 11:1-9

Just as God commanded Adam and Eve to be fruitful and multiply over the whole earth, He told Noah to do the same. But instead of multiplying and spreading over the whole earth, humanity chose to cluster together. Chronologically, the story of the tower of Babel fits sometime in the middle of Genesis 10—which gives us an account of the people who filled the earth. Before the people spread out speaking their own languages (Gen. 10:5), the following event took place.

The whole earth had the same language and vocabulary. As people migrated from the east, they found a valley in the land of Shinar and settled there. They said to each other, "Come, let us make oven-fired bricks." (They used brick for stone and asphalt for mortar.) And they said, "Come, let us build ourselves a city and a tower with its top in the sky. Let us make a name for ourselves; otherwise, we will be scattered throughout the earth." Then the LORD came down to look over the city and the tower that the humans were building. The LORD said, "If they have begun to do this as one people all having the same language, then nothing they plan to do will be impossible for them. Come, let's go down there and confuse their language so that they will not understand one another's speech." So from there the LORD scattered them throughout the earth, and they stopped building the city. Therefore it is called Babylon, for there the LORD confused the language of the whole earth, and from there the LORD scattered them throughout the earth.
GENESIS 11:1-9

Why did the people in Shinar want to build the tower to heaven? Why did God want to destroy it?

The people in this story wanted community, security, and identity. They wanted the community of a city. They wanted the security of a tower that would protect them from others. And they wanted their identity to come from a name for themselves. They wanted good things for the wrong reasons and by the wrong means. Every man wants a secure future, people who love him, and a purpose for his life. It's not wrong to want these things. But these guys wanted this for their own glory, and they were going to earn it themselves.

How have you tried to make a name for yourself in the wrong ways? What were the consequences of your actions?

When we build ourselves up, we go back to the root beneath Adam and Eve's sin. We say that we want to be the ones who decide what is good and evil. We want to be in charge. So God divided the people into multiple languages and "scattered them throughout the earth" (Gen. 11:8). Their desire to achieve community, security, and identity apart from God was halted. The people were also pushed outward, spread across the land as God commanded (Gen. 1:28; 9:7).

All this was in God's plan. Today, He doesn't receive worship in just one language, but many languages. And when His story concludes, He will be worshiped by people from every tribe, tongue, and nation (Rev. 5:9-10).

As we move forward to the next session, Genesis 12 will show us that God was going to bless all the nations through one man—a man willing to leave his community, his security, and his identity. He trusted God for all three instead of foolishly attempting to earn them on his own.

How have you found community in Christ? What about security? What about your identity?

2

SEASON 2

PROMISE & A PEOPLE

THE GOD OF ABRAHAM, ISAAC, AND JACOB

	2000 BC	1400 BC	1000 BC	600 BC	AD	AD 30	
CREATION & FALL	PROMISE & A PEOPLE	RESCUE & LAW	LAND & KINGDOM	EXILE & RETURN	JESUS	A NEW PEOPLE	A BETTER BEGINNING

It's a phrase used often throughout the Scripture: "the God of Abraham, the God of Isaac, and the God of Jacob." But who are they? And what does their story have to say about being a man?

At this point in the story, sin has ravaged humanity. But our good and gracious God never gives up on us. In the midst of our sin, God pursued His people—and He started with one family.

ABRAHAM

God promised Abraham something great—to make him the father of many nations. But the price was steep: He would have to leave his identity, his community, and his security behind. What did he do?

1. Abraham _left._

> Go out from your land, your relatives, and your father's house to the land that I will show you. I will make you into a great nation, I will bless you, I will make your name great, and you will be a blessing. I will bless those who bless you, I will curse anyone who treats you with contempt, and all the peoples on earth will be blessed through you.
> **GENESIS 12:1-3**

God told Abraham to give up his name, his security, and his community. Why do think He asked Abraham to make sacrifices in order to receive His blessings?

2. Abraham _slept._

> As the sun was setting, a deep sleep came over Abram, and suddenly great terror and darkness descended on him.
> **GENESIS 15:12**

> When the sun had set and it was dark, a smoking fire pot and a flaming torch appeared and passed between the divided animals. On that day the LORD made a covenant with Abram.
> **GENESIS 15:17-18A**

When God wanted to make a covenant with Abraham, Abraham fell asleep. Yet God made the covenant anyway for him. What does this say about God?

3. Abraham *laughed.*

> *The LORD came to Sarah as he had said, and the LORD did for Sarah what he had promised. Sarah became pregnant and bore a son to Abraham in his old age, at the appointed time God had told him. Abraham named his son who was born to him— the one Sarah bore to him—Isaac. When his son Isaac was eight days old, Abraham circumcised him, as God had commanded him. Abraham was a hundred years old when his son Isaac was born to him. Sarah said, "God has made me laugh, and everyone who hears will laugh with me."*
> **GENESIS 21:1-6**

Abraham doubted God could do something impossible—but He did it anyway. When have you seen God do something amazing?

ABRAHAM AND ISAAC

After giving him a son at 100 years old, God asked Abraham to make the ultimate sacrifice.

Read Genesis 22:7–14 out loud.

The essence of sin is man putting himself in the place of God. The essence of salvation is God putting Himself in our place. This story is pointing toward Jesus' death on the cross for us.

How is the story of Abraham and Isaac mirrored in the story of Jesus' death?

ABRAHAM, ISAAC, AND JACOB

Isaac's son, Jacob, deceived him in order to receive his older brother's inheritance. When he ran away in fear, God pursued him and came to him in a vision.

> *He reached a certain place and spent the night there because the sun had set. He took one of the stones from the place, put it there at his head, and lay down in that place. And he dreamed: A stairway was set on the ground with its top reaching the sky, and God's angels were going up and down on it. The LORD was standing there beside him, saying, "I am the LORD, the God of your father Abraham and the God of Isaac. I will give you and your offspring the land on which you are lying. Your offspring will be like the dust of the earth, and you will spread out toward the west, the east, the north, and the south. All the peoples on earth will be blessed through you and your offspring.*
> **GENESIS 28:11-14**

God repeats the promise he gave Abraham and Isaac here to Jacob. In doing so, He gives us a picture—not of a ladder that we can climb to God, but of a God who descends to us. The only way we are able to receive God's forgiveness is because Jesus came here for us.

> *And if you belong to Christ, then you are Abraham's seed, heirs according to the promise.*
> **GALATIANS 3:29**

What do the stories of Abraham, Isaac, and Jacob have to say about what it means to be a man?

How has God pursued you?

SEASON 2

PERSONAL BIBLE STUDY

The Christian faith is deeply connected to the family of Abraham. The God of Abraham, Isaac, and Jacob is also our God. From the lineage of Abraham comes Christ, and through Christ, people of all nations are made happy (blessed). Notice the timeline on page 26. Abraham, approximately 2,000 years before Christ, points us to Christ. Then after Christ was crucified, resurrected, and ascended back into heaven, the New Testament writers referenced Abraham in their letters. During your personal study this week, press in so you can see how the faith and the family of this one man unfolds throughout the Bible, takes us to Christ, and matters for you today.

DAY 1

SALVATION BY PROMISE

GALATIANS 3:15-18

When the apostle Paul wrote his letter to the church at Galatia, he was writing to people who were confused about how to become and live as a Christian. The confusion was about Christ vs. the law: The Galatian believers had received Christ as Lord, but they were being falsely taught that they also needed to keep the law that God gave to Moses. (We'll look closer at the law next week.)

In Galatians, Paul's message is clear: "You only need Christ." He uses the promise God gave Abraham to prove his point.

Look at the timeline on page 26. Which did God give first: the promise to Abraham or the law to Moses? Why is this important?

What's the difference between a covenant and a law? Why is this important when it comes to the gospel?

Now, read what Paul told the Galatians.

Brothers and sisters, I'm using a human illustration. No one sets aside or makes additions to a validated human will. Now the promises were spoken to Abraham and to his seed. He does not say "and to seeds," as though referring to many, but referring to one, and to your seed, who is Christ. My point is this: The law, which came 430 years later, does not invalidate a covenant previously established by God and thus cancel the promise. For if the inheritance is based on the law, it is no longer based on the promise; but God has graciously given it to Abraham through the promise.

GALATIANS 3:15-18

Think back to this week's Group Discussion. What was the promise God made to Abraham? "All nations will be blessed by your offspring." This wasn't the law—it was a promise. And because the promise came before the law, the law can't change it.

This promise is huge because it has eternal ramifications: God wasn't just laying out Abraham's family tree—He was announcing the gospel in advance. The offspring that brings the blessing to all nations is Christ.

> **Think back to a time you made a promise with someone. Why were you willing to bind yourself to them?**

It's important to see how this covenant came together in Genesis 15. Back then, when two people made a covenant, they would cut animals into pieces, spread them out on the ground, and walk through them together to signify the seriousness of the arrangement.

This symbolic action said, *if I break this covenant, may I be cut up like this animal was.* It was graphic, yes, but that's what made it serious. As both parties walked through the pieces together, they were saying, *I promise to fulfill my end of the deal—and if I don't, I am pronouncing judgment on myself.*

God and Abraham set this up in Genesis 15:9. But then when it came time for the covenant ritual to begin, something amazing happened: Abraham fell asleep. Stop here and read Genesis 15:12–18.

Did you see what happened in verse 17? When Abraham fell asleep, God did something incredible: He went it alone. He walked alone through the sacrifice, doing all the work Himself. Abraham was there, but he did nothing except believe. God alone fulfilled the promise—a promise that had nothing to do with Abraham's ability or his obedience. It was all about God's grace and faithfulness.

> **Why did God choose to walk through the ritual alone? How would it have been different if Abraham went alongside Him?**

We experience this same power through salvation through Christ. It's all God's work. Sadly, many guys don't really believe this. We're competitors. Achievers. We want to *win.* This can make us think we play a part in our salvation. But we don't. And that's what makes it beautiful.

A recent study by LifeWay Research found that 71 percent of Americans believe they must contribute something to their salvation.[2] This is tragic, because it undermines God's entire sacrifice. To think we played a part in saving ourselves is to not rely fully on His grace, on Christ. Like Abraham, we were asleep. We could not fulfill our part of the covenant. We were dead in our sins, but God who is rich in mercy made us alive in Christ (Eph. 2:1-5).

The English preacher William Temple said it well: "The only thing of my very own which I contribute to my redemption is the sin from which I need to be redeemed."[3]

When was a time you found yourself trying to earn God's favor? What happened?

So you may be wondering, *if we are only saved because of the promise that Christ would come, then what's the purpose of the law?* Paul anticipated this question and gave the answer:

> *Why then was the law given? It was added for the sake of transgressions until the Seed to whom the promise was made would come.*
> **GALATIANS 3:19**

The law came to point us to Christ. It's what shows us we are sinful and need Christ to rescue us. If we receive Christ and put our trust in Him, we are heirs of the promise. We belong to Christ and are part of Abraham's family. Remember the song you used to sing in church as a kid? "Father Abraham had many sons, and many sons had father Abraham. I am one of them…" Pretty deep for a 6-year-old, but it's true. If your faith is in Christ, you are in Abraham's family. It's your faith that makes you right with God—not your race, your social status, your grades, or your championships. Only Christ.

> *There is no Jew or Greek, slave or free, male or female; since you are all one in Christ Jesus. And if you belong to Christ, then you are Abraham's seed, heirs according to the promise.*
> **GALATIANS 3:28-29**

Take a moment to thank God for His covenant with us and the promise of Jesus. Let Him know what this means to you personally and how it's changed your life.

SAVED JUST LIKE ABRAHAM

ROMANS 4:1-5

Maybe you're thinking, *OK, I get that we are now saved by believing in Christ. But what about those people who lived before Christ came?*

Some people think that those who lived before Christ were saved by their deeds, and now we are saved by our faith. But that can't be true, because if you could be saved by your deeds, then why did we need Christ at all? No, we are saved by looking back to the cross and placing our faith in Christ. Those who lived before Christ were saved by looking forward to it and placing their faith in God's promise. We see this in Abraham's life. He did not earn God's favor; He simply believed the Lord, and his faith was credited as righteousness (Gen. 15:6).

> **How do you often hear the word "credit" used? What do you think it means then to "credit" righteousness?**

It is an incredible phrase. Paul brings it back in Romans when he uses Abraham's faith as an example of what happens when someone becomes a Christian.

> *What then will we say that Abraham, our forefather according to the flesh, has found? If Abraham was justified by works, he has something to boast about—but not before God. For what does the Scripture say? Abraham believed God, and it was credited to him for righteousness. Now to the one who works, pay is not credited as a gift, but as something owed. But to the one who does not work, but believes on Him who declares the ungodly to be righteous, his faith is credited for righteousness.*
> **ROMANS 4:1-5**

When Abraham placed his faith in God, God declared him to be righteous, meaning that Abraham was justified and made right with God. To be justified and to be made righteous essentially mean the same thing, deriving from the same root word in the biblical language.

Think for a second about what it means to be made right with God. It's like God hitting "undo" on everything you've ever done. All your sin—washed away. All your mistakes— forgiven. A blank page. A new start. What a gift.

Even if you've placed your faith in Jesus, you can still ask for a new start by asking for forgiveness. Think about the different areas of your life and walk through these statements in prayer.

I need a new start when it comes to my _____.

This is a struggle for me because _____.

I need God to help me _____.

I can pray specifically for Him to _____.

When you stop working to earn your salvation—when you stop trying to stand before God in your own goodness and trust Him instead—you are justified. You are made righteous.

Just as Abraham received righteousness by placing his faith in God, so do we. Not by our own efforts. Only through God.

Think of a time you tried to earn your own salvation. Why is God's way a better way?

Grab some paper and write down five short prayers—just one or two lines each, thanking God or asking for His help. Pray one a day for the rest of the week, trusting in Him to make you righteous.

ISAAC AS AN ILLUSTRATION

GALATIANS 4:21-31

Have you ever heard a really awesome testimony? You know—some guy who talks on stage about how he got addicted to drugs, stole thousands of dollars, ran from the cops, and escaped from a gang before giving his life to the Lord and turning over a new leaf.

It might sound a little intense compared to yours. Maybe you were raised in a great Christian family, singing Chris Tomlin on the way to church with your parents and serving the Lord every week. It can make you feel more dull than radical.

But here's the thing—*every* testimony is radical, because every person who knows Jesus has been radically saved. None of us were deader in sin than anyone else, and none of us have been made any more alive than another. We were supernaturally born of God, not because of anything we did but because of His promise.

On a scale of 1–10, how "radical" do you think your testimony is? Have you ever envied someone else's testimony?

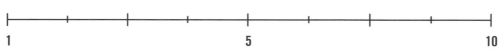

1   5   10

Being a Christian isn't just radical—it's supernatural. When you become a Christian, you are supernaturally born of God. The apostle Paul walks us through it in Galatians, using the birth of Isaac as an illustration. This is a great example of why we need to look at the Bible as one whole story rather than as a collection—Paul is bringing the Old and New Testaments together here by reaching back to make a point about God's grace through Christ.

> *Tell me, those of you who want to be under the law, don't you hear the law? For it is written that Abraham had two sons, one by a slave and the other by a free woman. But the one by the slave was born as a result of the flesh, while the one by the free woman was born through promise. ... Now you too, brothers and sisters, like Isaac, are children of promise. But just as then the child born as a result of the flesh persecuted the one born as a result of the Spirit, so also now. But what does the Scripture say? "Drive out the slave and her son, for the son of the slave will never be a coheir with the son of the free woman." Therefore, brothers and sisters, we are not children of the slave but of the free woman.*
> **GALATIANS 4:21-23,28–31**

There is a lot going on in this passage, so maybe this chart will help:

THE LAW	GRACE
Abraham & Hagar	Abraham & Sarah
Ishmael	Isaac

Abraham and Sarah longed for a child. God promised them that they would have one, but as time passed, Sarah lost hope. In her impatience, she told her husband to sleep with one of her servants, Hagar. Abraham agreed to the plan, resulting in Hagar becoming pregnant. Hagar bore Abraham a son, and he named him Ishmael.

When was a time you got impatient with God? What happened?

At this point, some might think God would write Abraham and Sarah off for not believing the promise, for taking matters into their own hands. But God did what He said He would do despite Abraham and Sarah's lack of faith. Though they were faithless, He remained faithful. Years passed, and Sarah finally got pregnant. The couple named their son Isaac.

The two circumstances were very different. Ishmael was the result of Abraham and Hagar trusting themselves rather than God. They couldn't wait for God's promise to be fulfilled. Isaac, however, was the result of God's promise. Abraham and Sarah were way past child-bearing years, so only in God's power were they able to have a child. It was supernatural in that it was the work of God, not the work of man.

The two children were very different from one another. Ishmael was the son of a slave. Isaac was the son of God's promise.

If you are a Christian, then you are a son of that same promise. That's a radical testimony. You aren't a slave. You have been born of God. You are a miracle because you were dead in your sins, and God made you alive in Him. You were supernaturally brought to God because of His grace, not because you earned it. That's your story, man. Own it and go tell it.

Write out your testimony, emphasizing the supernatural aspect of God's salvation.

ABRAHAM'S EXAMPLE

HEBREWS 11:8-10

As you have seen so far this week, the apostle Paul took readers back to the story of Abraham in his letter to churches. But he wasn't the only New Testament writer to do so. Matthew, James, Peter, and the writer of Hebrews mention Abraham as well. In both Hebrews and James, we see Abraham's faith held up as example.

We have learned that Abraham was made right with God because of God, that he was not perfect and struggled just like we do. But we also see what faith looks like in this world, how we should live now that we have been made right with God. Today, study several of these passages and wrestle with the questions that follow.

> *By faith Abraham, when he was called, obeyed and set out for a place that he was going to receive as an inheritance. He went out, even though he did not know where he was going. By faith he stayed as a foreigner in the land of promise, living in tents as did Isaac and Jacob, coheirs of the same promise. For he was looking forward to the city that has foundations, whose architect and builder is God.*
> **HEBREWS 11:8-10**

Abraham gave up all the comforts of home and left everything to obey God. Faith always requires sacrifice, big and small. So what have you given up to follow God? What has your faith cost you?

Verse 10 gives us insight into what motivated Abraham to give up so much: *"For he was looking forward to the city that has foundations, whose architect and builder is God."* He was looking to the next life, not this one. The only way we can give up things in this world is if we believe in and long for the next one.

> *By faith Abraham, when he was tested, offered up Isaac. He received the promises and yet he was offering his one and only son, the one to whom it had been said, Your offspring will be called through Isaac. He considered God to be able even to raise someone from the dead; therefore, he received him back, figuratively speaking.*
> **HEBREWS 11:17-19**

This is a staggering story. God made a huge promise to Abraham through Isaac, and then told Abraham to sacrifice him. What? Why would God do something like that?

The point was to see who was on the throne of Abraham's life: Was it his son, or was it God? Abraham lifted the knife to his boy because "he considered God to be able even to raise someone from the dead" (Heb. 11:19). In other words, Abraham had no idea what was about to happen, but he knew God was good. He trusted Him. He believed God's promise to the point that if Isaac was killed, he knew God could raise him from the dead. What an incredible faith.

God wants us to give up sinful things to follow Him. But look at this story—he also wants to be above the good things we love. Think about the things you love—what are the things you need to constantly be sure don't become gods in your heart?

But someone will say, "You have faith, and I have works." Show me your faith without works, and I will show you faith by my works. You believe that God is one. Good! Even the demons believe—and they shudder. Senseless person! Are you willing to learn that faith without works is useless? Wasn't Abraham our father justified by works in offering Isaac his son on the altar? You see that faith was active together with his works, and by works, faith was made complete, and the Scripture was fulfilled that says, Abraham believed God, and it was credited to him for righteousness, and he was called God's friend.
JAMES 2:18-23

Remember from earlier that the apostle Paul pointed out that Abraham was justified only by his faith. But this passage seems to say that Abraham was justified by his works. This can seem confusing or contradictory, but you have to look at the context.

Look at James 2:18 once again: *"I will show you faith by my works."* Works never lead to faith—remember, you can't earn your salvation—but faith always leads to works. Of course it does! If we have true faith, our lives show it. If we have true faith, we'll want to show it. That's the power of Abraham's story: Abraham believed God, received God's righteousness, and then showed he had true faith by being willing to offer his son. There's an old saying: "We are saved by faith alone, but the faith that saves is never alone." Faith and works go together—and true faith always takes action.

Who is someone you know who shows their faith through their actions? How is this person using their life as a platform for Christ?

3

SEASON 3

RESCUE & LAW

BURNING BUSH, BLOODY DOORPOSTS, A MOUNTAIN AND A TENT

CREATION & FALL	PROMISE & A PEOPLE	RESCUE & LAW	LAND & KINGDOM	EXILE & RETURN	JESUS	A NEW PEOPLE	A BETTER BEGINNING
	2000 BC	1400 BC	1000 BC	600 BC	AD	AD 30	

The story of Moses isn't just a story of deliverance. It also reveals a lot about God. Here are three ways God reveals His character in this story.

1. GOD DELIVERS

> *Then Moses asked God, "If I go to the Israelites and say to the, 'The God of your fathers has sent me to you,' and they ask me, 'What is his name?' what should I tell them?" God replied to Moses, "I AM WHO I AM. This is what you are to say to the Israelites: I AM has sent me to you." God also said to Moses, "Say this to the Israelites: The Lord, the God of your fathers, the God of Abraham, the God of Isaac, and the God of Jacob, has sent me to you. This is my name forever; this is how I am to be remembered in every generation."*
> **EXODUS 3:13-15**

After God revealed Himself to Moses in the burning bush, He sent a series of plagues upon Egypt, including a promise to murder all firstborn sons across the land whose houses were not covered in the blood of a lamb.

> *"I will pass through the land of Egypt on that night and strike every firstborn male in the land of Egypt, both people and animals. I am the Lord; I will execute judgments against all the gods of Egypt. The blood on the houses where you are staying will be a distinguishing mark for you; when I see the blood, I will pass over you. No plague will be among you to destroy you when I strike the land of Egypt."*
> **EXODUS 12:12-13**
>
> **God makes two promises here: one to Moses and one to Egypt. He keeps them both. When has God kept a promise with you?**

2. GOD DIRECTS

> *Moses went up the mountain to God, and the Lord called to him from the mountain: "This is what you must say to the house of Jacob and explain to the Israelites: 'You have seen what I did to the Egyptians and how I carried you on eagles' wings and brought you to myself. Now if you will carefully listen to me and keep my covenant, you will be my own possession out of all the peoples, although all the whole earth is mine, and you will be my kingdom of priests and my holy nation.' These are the words that you are to say to the Israelites.*
> **EXODUS 19:3-6**

After God delivered His people, He directed them through the law.

> *I am the LORD your God, who brought you out of the land of Egypt, out of the place of slavery. Do not have other gods besides me.*
> **EXODUS 20:2-3**

What do you think of when you hear the word "law"? How does God want us to think about it?

3. GOD DWELLS

> *The cloud covered the tent of meeting, and the glory of the LORD filled the tabernacle. Moses was unable to enter the tent of meeting because the cloud rested on it, and the glory of the LORD filled the tabernacle. The Israelites set out whenever the cloud was taken up from the tabernacle throughout all the stages of their journey. If the cloud was not taken up, they did not set out until the day it was taken up. For the cloud of the LORD was over the tabernacle by day, and there was a fire inside the cloud by night, visible to the entire house of Israel throughout all the stages of their journey.*
> **EXODUS 40:34-38**

After delivering His people from slavery, God promised His people He was still with them. He hadn't left them. He was dwelling among them.

Why is it important that God stayed with His people after delivering them, rather than abandoning them?

The stories of the Old Testament are always pointing to Jesus. Here are five things we learn about Jesus from these stories:

Jesus is:

1. The <u>I AM.</u>

> *Jesus said to them, "Truly I tell you, before Abraham was, I am."*
> **JOHN 8:58**

2. The <u>Lamb.</u>

> *The next day John saw Jesus coming toward him and said, "Here is the Lamb of God, who takes away the sin of the world!*
> **JOHN 1:29**

3. The fulfillment of the <u>Law.</u>

> *"Don't think that I came to abolish the Law or the Prophets. I did not come to abolish but to fulfill."*
> **MATTHEW 5:17**

4. The <u>tabernacle.</u>

> *The Word became flesh and dwelt among us. We observed his glory, the glory as the one and only Son from the Father, full of grace and truth.*
> **JOHN 1:14**

5. The greater <u>Moses.</u>

> *For Jesus is considered worthy of more glory than Moses.*
> **HEBREWS 3:3A**

Part of being a man is learning how to be a leader. What do we learn about leadership from Moses' story?

What does it mean that Jesus is "the greater Moses"?

How is God calling you to follow Him today? What do you have in your life that you need to give over to Him?

SEASON 3

PERSONAL BIBLE STUDY

During the first three days of
this week's personal study we
will zoom in on the timeline
of events we covered in the
Season 3 teaching: Moses
receiving the law, man's inability to
keep it, and thus man's need for
a priest and sacrifices. Then the
last day will take us forward in the
storyline to God's people entering
the land God had promised them.

THE TEN COMMANDMENTS

EXODUS 20

When you think of the Ten Commandments, what comes to mind? Maybe you think of a teacher standing at the front of the room, taking names on the board. Or maybe you think of a referee watching over you during a game, waiting on you to commit a penalty so you can be punished. Whatever it is, you probably think of rules. And rules aren't fun. Which is why we have a distorted view of the Ten Commandments.

God gave the Ten Commandments to people He graciously and miraculously delivered from slavery. The commandments weren't merely a set of holy rules they were expected to follow at all times—they were given to God's people in response to who God is and the rescue He provided.

What are the strictest rules you have to follow? Why do you think they were set that way?

I am the LORD your God, who brought you out of the land of Egypt, out of the place of slavery. Do not have other gods besides me. Do not make an idol for yourself, whether in the shape of anything in the heavens above or on the earth below or in the waters under the earth. Do not bow in worship to them, and do not serve them; for I, the LORD your God, am a jealous God, punishing the children for the fathers' iniquity, to the third and fourth generations of those who hate me.
EXODUS 20:2-5

WHO GOD IS: "I AM THE LORD YOUR GOD"

He is the One who is above all others, the Creator and Sustainer, the God above all gods and the King above all kings.

WHAT HE HAS DONE: "WHO BROUGHT YOU OUT OF THE LAND OF EGYPT"

He is the One who rescued the people from their slavery, from the shame of being mistreated and abused, from the disgrace of being owned by the Egyptians. The Ten Commandments were given in response to their rescue from slavery, and they simultaneously pointed to the Rescuer (Jesus) who would come to deliver us from our sins. They point us to Jesus because the Commandments show us we need Jesus. We can't keep them on our own—we need Him to keep them for us, to change our hearts, and to forgive us our sins.

The same is true for you. God's commands are given to you because of who God is and because He has rescued you from the slavery of sin.

How do the Ten Commandments point forward to the coming Christ?

Scholars often divide the Ten Commandments into two broad sections: commandments about our relationship with God and commandments about our relationships with other people. Read Exodus 20:1-17, then take a shot at dividing the commandments up in the two categories below.

LOVE FOR GOD	LOVE FOR OTHERS

Want the answers? The first four commandments deal with our relationship with God, and the following six deal with our relationships with one another.

The first commandment is a big one, because it speaks about our hearts only bowing to the God who has rescued us. We shall have no other god—no other thing—besides Him in our hearts. He alone should rule and reign in our hearts because He alone rules and reigns over all things, and He alone has rescued us.

Martin Luther taught that if we break any of the commandments it is because we have already broken the first commandment, and if we keep the first commandment, we will keep all the others. For example, if we steal (violating the eighth commandment), it is only because we put the thing we are stealing ahead of God in our hearts. If we commit adultery, it is because we have put the pursuit of a woman ahead of God in our hearts. If we don't honor our parents, it is because we have stopped honoring our Father in our hearts.

The way we are motivated to keep the first commandment is to continually be in awe that He is the Lord our God who brought us "out of the place of slavery" (Ex. 20:2). When we lose this awe, the commandments begin to look like a burden. But as we have more awe, we will want to obey Him because we love Him. This is love for God: to obey His commands, and His commands are not burdensome (1 John 5:3).

When does obeying God's commands feel burdensome to you? Why?

Take a few minutes to reflect on the great salvation that Christ has purchased for you. Consider the sacrifice He made and where you would be without Him. Let the awe and wonder of His great love fill your heart today.

BROKEN PROMISES ALREADY

EXODUS 32

Imagine you're a teenager trapped in slavery in Egypt. You're an Israelite—one of God's chosen people—but all around you, your people plead for deliverance. Every night, your parents pray for rescue. You work for an Egyptian family for no pay and no gratitude. You barely see your father because he works for the Pharaoh from sunup to sundown, every day, with no relief.

One day, a guy named Moses begins speaking to a crowd outside your house. He says that God told him to tell the leader of Egypt to set Israel free. You hear about this land promised to Abraham, Isaac, and Jacob. You long to leave Egypt and leave slavery behind, but this seems so random and so completely unlikely.

But then Moses promises God will send plagues—and soon you start to see them. One after another, the supernatural starts to happen all around you. *Wow*, you think, *this may actually be happening.*

You help your father put blood on the doors in preparation for the final plague. You struggle to sleep that night, anticipating what's to come. Late in the night you wake to wailing and crying throughout the city. Those without the blood of lambs on their doorposts lose their firstborn sons. It's surreal, but you don't have time to process it—it's time to flee.

There is great urgency and excitement among your people, shouting up and down the streets. The Egyptians are actually begging you to leave. They are terrified of displeasing your God anymore. So you ask them for their possessions, as Moses instructed, and they actually give them to you. You leave Egypt with their gold and their silver. The gift of freedom is greater, but the gifts of gold and silver remind you that God has orchestrated all of this. The God of Abraham, Isaac, and Jacob is your God, too, and He liberated you.

After rushing out of Egypt you come to the Red Sea. And as some feared, Pharaoh and the Egyptians are furiously pursuing you. In the distance, you see Moses lift up his hands, as the waters of the sea lift into the sky and split in two. It's the loudest noise you've ever heard—the most terrifying thing you've ever seen—but it's also clear that God is making a way for you to cross to safety.

When you cross and turn around, the waters fall on the Egyptians. Everyone cheers. You stand in awe of the God who brought this about.

A few months later, Moses comes down from a mountain where He had met with the Lord. You are eager to hear from the One who liberated you, who loved and protected you. Moses gives God's first commandment:

> I am the LORD your God, who brought you out of the land of Egypt, out of the place of slavery. Do not have other gods besides me.
> **EXODUS 20:2-3**

He then gives the second command:

> Do not make an idol for yourself, whether in the shape of anything in the heavens above or on the earth below or in the waters under the earth. Do not bow in worship to them, and do not serve them; for I, the LORD your God, am a jealous God.
> **EXODUS 20:4-5A**

Of course! You nod as you commit in your heart to give God and only God your worship. Only He deserves it. Only He has rescued me, you say to yourself.

Read Exodus 32:1-8 to see what happened.

After being rescued by God, the people find something other than God to worship. They take the gold the Lord gave them—the gifts from the Egyptians—and make a golden calf to honor, to give credit for their rescue from slavery.

What are you idolizing in your life? How does this go against God's commands?

Whenever we look to something other than God to give us our worth or satisfaction, we are committing the same sin of idolatry. Baseball, a girl, the guitar, your car—anything can be an idol. When we abandon the One who has rescued us for something less than Him, we are bowing down to an idol, to something created and not the Creator. Everything that is not Him pales in comparison to the God who can say, "I am the LORD your God who brought you out of slavery. Do not have other gods besides me."

Why did the Israelites make a false idol when it was so obvious how God had rescued them?

In the space below, write out a brief prayer to God asking forgiveness for the times you have placed something before Him in your life. Name it specifically, then ask Him to help you keep his commands. Give thanks for His rescue, His grace, and His promises.

PRIESTS, SACRIFICES, AND THE DAY OF ATONEMENT

LEVITICUS 16

Shortly after God gave His people the Ten Commandments in Exodus 20—including the commandments to not worship another god or make a false idol—His people were already bowing down to a golden calf. So God, in His mercy, set up a sacrificial system that would allow sinful man to approach our holy God.

God instituted an elaborate system where priests would offer bloody sacrifices to God to serve as a temporary covering of sin. Every day, priests were busy offering sacrifices for themselves and for others: In the Book of Leviticus, we find burnt offerings, sin offerings, grain offerings, fellowship offerings, and guilt offerings. The detailed instructions for sacrifices and offerings pointed people to the holiness of God and the reality that we cannot approach Him in our own merit.

All the sacrifices were designed to teach the people to loathe sin. Constant sacrifices meant people were confronted continually with the seriousness of sin. All the bloody sacrifices, all the screaming of animals, would cause the people to hate their sin, to think, *My sin causes death. Every time I sin something dies.*

> **Think of a time recently when you made a mistake and you knew it. How do you think God wants to use those moments?**

The sacrificial system would help people long for a Savior. The constant sacrifices reminded the people that they could not rescue themselves or cleanse themselves. They needed a Savior whose blood was more sufficient than the blood of an animal.

All the daily sacrifices still were not enough, so God commanded a special Day of Atonement to be remembered annually.

Read Leviticus 16:1-10.

On the Day of Atonement, God instructed that two goats would be set apart. One of the goats would be slaughtered to signify that God's wrath was poured out on the sacrifice instead of on His people. The priest took the blood from the goat, brought it into the Most Holy Place inside the tabernacle, and sprinkled the blood on the lid of the Ark of the Covenant, also known as the mercy seat. Inside the Ark, the Ten Commandments were stored. The people—just as we have—sinned against His law. So the blood being sprinkled on the mercy seat signified that God's wrath was being turned from His people and placed on the goat instead. Mercy was triumphing over judgment.

Why do you think it's important that blood was used in these ceremonies? What does it signify?

The second goat, however, was not killed. Instead of killing this goat, the priest would put his hands on the goat to symbolize that the sins of the people were transferred to the goat. The goat was then led to the wilderness and set free, symbolizing that the sins of the people were cast away from them. They were forgiven, because God's holy wrath was appeased.

One sacrifice symbolized that the wrath of God was satisfied. The other symbolized the sins of the people being removed from them.

When Jesus came hundreds of years later, He perfectly fulfilled the function of both sacrifices. When He placed Himself on the cross—willingly laying down His life for us—He placed Himself on the sacrificial altar. His body absorbed the wrath that should be ours, the wrath that we deserve. He removed our sin from us.

The people could not keep God's commands, so an elaborate sacrificial system allowed them to approach God and enjoy His dwelling among them. We could not keep His commands either, so Jesus came as our sacrifice.

Why were these Old Testament sacrifices not sufficient to forgive our sins? How is Jesus the perfect sacrifice?

Read the story of Jesus' crucifixion in Matthew 27. What are the parallels to the sacrifices of Leviticus?

VICTORY WITHOUT A FIGHT

JOSHUA 6:1-21

When God chose Moses to lead His people to freedom, He not only promised their liberation from slavery—He also promised He would give them the land promised to their forefathers Abraham, Isaac, and Jacob (Ex. 6:2-8).

After wandering the desert for 40 years, God's people were ready to move into the land of Canaan, the promised land. But there was one problem: the land wasn't vacant. Other people lived there, and those people needed to be conquered. God promised to drive out the other people not only because of His love for Israel, but also because of the wickedness of those living in Canaan (Deut. 9:4-5). The people living there were wicked and they were not conquered until their sin "reached its full measure" before God (Gen. 15:16).

Moses' successor, Joshua, was the man God used to lead the people to conquer the land and divide it among God's people. But really God was the One who secured the victory. The first battle on the conquest made this absolutely clear. God handed over Jericho, a city in Canaan, to His people—to the nation of Israel. Without the Israelites raising a fist, God already called the battle: "I have handed Jericho to … you" (Josh. 6:2).

Read Joshua 6:1-21. Circle three words in your Bible that jump out to you, or write them in the margins here. Why did you choose them?

Priests carried the Ark of the Covenant around the city walls, leading the way with seven trumpets. Troops marched in front and behind the Ark, but they didn't do a thing—not even shout. For six days they did this. On the seventh day, Joshua told the people to shout when they heard the trumpets blast. When they shouted, the walls crumbled. God gave Jericho to His people.

The story reminds us that God wants to use our weakness. As men, we want to be strong. When you walk on the football field, you want to conquer. When you step on the court, you want to dominate. When you step in the batter's box, you want glory. But in God's kingdom, strength is found in our weakness. It sounds contradictory—impossible, really—but it's true.

When we realize we are weak compared to Him, and that we, in our ability, cannot stand strong, God is attracted to our humility. He knows the proud from a distance, but the humble He knows up close (Ps. 138:6). Though we want to fight battles in our own strength, we must learn to walk quietly and allow the Lord to crumble the walls that He wants to crumble.

> **Michael Jordan once said, "I've missed more than 9,000 shots in my career. I've lost almost 300 games. Twenty-six times, I've been trusted to take the game winning shot and missed. I've failed over and over and over again in my life. And that is why I succeed."[4] Why does this sound like success to him?**

> **What examples can you think of in Scripture where God used someone's weakness?**

God continued to give every city in Canaan to His people. They moved into the land, divided it, and were finally home—finally to the place the Lord had promised His people, first to Abraham, Isaac, and Jacob.

When they were in the land, the Lord reminded the people that He gave them the land and the victory. As Joshua reminded the people of their history, the Lord declared:

> *"I gave you a land you did not labor for, and cities you did not build, though you live in them; you are eating from vineyards and olive groves you did not plant. Therefore, fear the LORD and worship Him in sincerity and truth. Get rid of the gods your fathers worshiped ..."*
> **JOSHUA 24:13-14**

Because the Lord has rescued us, defeated sin for us, and fulfilled every single promise He has made, we are to fear Him and worship Him. And we are to get rid of the little gods that clutter our lives.

> **What little gods are cluttering your life? Take a moment to ask God to replace them with Christ in your life.**

4

SEASON 4

LAND & KINGDOM

JUDGES, GODS,
AND KINGS

CREATION & FALL	PROMISE & A PEOPLE	RESCUE & LAW	LAND & KINGDOM	EXILE & RETURN	JESUS	A NEW PEOPLE	A BETTER BEGINNING
	2000 BC	1400 BC	1000 BC	600 BC	AD	AD 30	

Through seasons of sin, slavery, rescue, and deliverance, God kept making promises to His people—and every time He kept them. When God promises something, He delivers.

Here are three things we learn about God in this season of the Bible story:

1. GOD DELIVERS ON HIS PROMISES

So the LORD gave Israel all the land He had sworn to give their fathers, and they took possession of it and settled there. The LORD gave them rest on every side according to all he had sworn to their fathers. None of their enemies were able to stand against them, for the LORD handed over all their enemies to them. None of the good promises the LORD had made to the house of Israel failed. Everything was fulfilled.
JOSHUA 21:43-45

I gave you a land you did not labor for, and cities you did not build, though you live in them; you are eating from vineyards and olive groves you did not plant.
JOSHUA 24:13

In Joshua, God reminds His people that everything they have is from Him. Look at the actions God takes in these passages: "the Lord *gave*" and "the Lord *handed*." There's nothing we can do that would keep Him from delivering on what He promises.

What are some examples of things God promises us? How have you seen them come true in your life?

When was a time you promised someone something and didn't deliver? What happened?

2. GOD DISCIPLINES HIS PEOPLE

Read Judges 2:8, then verses 10-19.

God commanded His people to only worship Him. But as we've learned, we can't help but worship our own idols. We squander the good things He gives us. We want to rule ourselves. When God disciplines us, He does it because He loves us. He knows we won't be satisfied if we're worshiping other gods. So to get their attention, God disciplined His people, because He always disciplines those He loves.

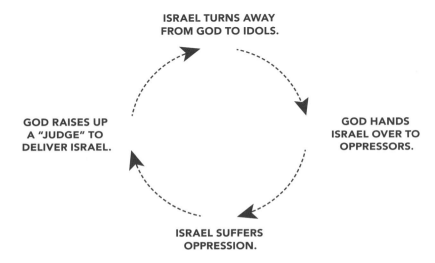

ISRAEL TURNS AWAY FROM GOD TO IDOLS.

GOD HANDS ISRAEL OVER TO OPPRESSORS.

ISRAEL SUFFERS OPPRESSION.

GOD RAISES UP A "JUDGE" TO DELIVER ISRAEL.

This cycle of sin happens over and over in our own lives. We turn to the same sin time and time again. God disciplines us, we turn to Him for a little while, but we always go back. We will stay stuck in this cycle unless we set our affection on Christ, who is above all.

> *Endure suffering as discipline: God is dealing with you as sons. For what son is there that a father does not discipline? But if you are without discipline—which all receive—then you are illegitimate children and not sons.*
> **HEBREWS 12:7-8**

When was a time you experienced severe discipline? What did you learn from it?

Why is discipline an important part of being a man? What would happen without it?

3. GOD DECLARES HIS PURPOSES

Read 2 Samuel 7:8-16.

Like He did with Abraham, God promises David something amazing: a kingdom that will live forever. That must have sounded pretty appealing to a king. But David was just a man—he couldn't live forever. From David's lineage, God was telling him, would come Jesus. It's right there in the first words of the New Testament:

> *An account of the genealogy of Jesus Christ, the Son of David, the Son of Abraham.*
> **MATTHEW 1:1**

God's love is a faithful love.

What kind of future do you think God wants for you?

What do you think you want to do with your life, and how can you worship Him through it?

PERSONAL BIBLE STUDY

In the Season 4 group discussion, we covered a lot of ground, from God's people moving into the promised land to the period of the judges. We also covered the reigns of Saul, David, and Solomon as kings of Israel. During this latter period in Israel's history, David wrote many of the psalms, and Solomon wrote Ecclesiastes, some of Proverbs, and Song of Solomon. This week's personal Bible study will give you a sampling of how this wisdom literature points to Jesus.

AN IMPERFECT KING

PSALM 51

The background to Psalm 51 is found in 2 Samuel 11–12. David had been a great leader, a man after God's own heart. He was a just and compassionate king. But he made a grave mistake that spiraled out of control.

Second Samuel 11 opens with David alone in Jerusalem, choosing to stay behind while his men go off to war. David was restless. Instead of "gazing on the beauty of the Lord" (Ps. 27:4), he went to the roof and watched a married woman named Bathsheba take a bath. He brought her to his room, slept with her, and she got pregnant.

Instead of coming clean about his sin, David doubled down and planned an elaborate cover-up. He brought her husband, Uriah, home from war, believing Uriah and Bathsheba would sleep together and no one would be the wiser. But Uriah refused to go home to his wife because his fellow soldiers were sleeping on battlefields. So David sent instructions to the battlefield that Uriah was to be sent onto the field where the fighting was fiercest, and then the troops were to be removed. Uriah was subsequently killed, and David had one-upped his adultery with murder.

> **David's trouble started when he wasn't where he was supposed to be—in battle with his men. When was a time you got in trouble because you were somewhere you weren't supposed to be?**

Nathan, the prophet, confronted David in his sin with an epic illustration: Hey David, a rich man has an out-of-town guest and instead of killing one of his many animals for supper, he kills the one lamb of a poor man. David burned with anger and wanted to find this man and administer justice. Nathan responded simply, "You are the man!" (2 Sam. 12:7). David, because he belonged to the Lord, recognized his sin, repented, and sought God for forgiveness. Psalm 51 is his prayer of forgiveness.

Read Psalm 51.

Notice that David did not pray for his eyes in this psalm. He did not pray that God would protect him from looking at women, nor that the Lord would give him friends who would hold him accountable. He did not make bold promises to God that he would never sin again. He knew he was too broken to keep a promise like that. Instead, he prayed for God to clean his heart (v. 10). He knew his heart was the problem.

Psalm 51 shows us the depth of sin in our hearts. It reveals to us just how much in need of God's grace we are. In the first two verses, we see three different words that give us a comprehensive view of our sin.

> *Be gracious to me, God, according to your faithful love; according to your abundant compassion, blot out my rebellion. Completely wash away my guilt and cleanse me from my sin. For I am conscious of my rebellion, and my sin is always before me.*
> **PSALM 51:1-2**

The three words describing the sinful depth of our hearts are:

1. REBELLION

In the original language, this word speaks of willful disobedience against the One to whom we owe our allegiance. Rebellion is our declaration to God that we will do things our way, not His. When David knew Bathsheba was married but pursued her anyway, this was rebellion.

2. GUILT

Guilt brings with it a sense of shifting. Our hearts have shifted out of place. Instead of focusing on Him, we focus on lesser things. David, as he walked around one night, was looking for something other than God; therefore, he was susceptible to the beauty of a woman.

Take a moment and think about the "lesser things" you've focused on this week. What has gotten in the way of you thinking about God?

3. SIN

Sin means to miss the mark. When we sin, we miss the mark of God's holiness. When David lusted, he missed the mark of God's love. When he lied, he missed the mark of God's truthfulness. When he murdered, he missed the mark of God who is life.

The good news is that God is eager to forgive, blot out our rebellion, wash away our guilt, and cleanse us from our sin. Our sin is great, but God's grace is greater.

David's sin reminds us that, though he was a great king, he was still imperfect and broken. We all are, even the king who unified Israel and conquered their enemies. Thankfully another King came from the line of David—the perfect and conquering King, Jesus, who secured our forgiveness on the cross.

David's story is about adultery, conspiracy, and murder—heavy topics, to be sure. But when we look to why David made the choices he did, we see a heart not too different than ours. Why did David keep trying to protect himself rather than come clean? How are we similar?

If you have unconfessed sin in your life, take time now to confess it to the Lord and ask Him to create in you a clean heart.

DAY 2

THE JOY OF FORGIVENESS

PSALM 32

The Psalms were compiled over hundreds of years and are not presented in chronological order. Though the 32nd Psalm comes before Psalm 51 in our Bibles, scholars believe that Psalm 32 is David's celebration of his forgiveness after he prayed Psalm 51. So the order of these events is:

> David's sin (2 Sam. 11) > Nathan's confrontation (2 Sam. 12) > David's confession (Ps. 51) > David's celebration (Ps. 32)

Read Psalm 32.

Yesterday we studied three words in Psalm 51 that show us the depth of our sin. In this psalm, we see three words that show us the greatness of our forgiveness. David was overwhelmed with the awesomeness of God's forgiveness. Here's what Charles Spurgeon had to say about this wonderful passage:

"Note the three words often used to denote our disobedience: transgression, sin, and iniquity are the three-headed dog at the gates of hell, but our glorious Lord has silenced its barkings forever against his own believing ones. The trinity of sin is overcome by the Trinity of heaven."[5]

The three words are found in the first two verses:

> How joyful is the one whose transgression is forgiven, whose sin is covered! How joyful is a person whom the LORD does not charge with iniquity and in whose spirit is no deceit!
> **PSALM 32:1-2**

1. FORGIVEN

The word for forgiven in the original Hebrew (the Old Testament was originally written in Hebrew) means "carried away." Your sin, if you are His, has been carried away. If you, in your mind, are still carrying sin from your past—you are carrying a mirage. Your sin is no longer with you; instead, the Lord has carried it away.

A mirage is something illusory, without substance or reality. What is your response to knowing your past sins are not real anymore?

2. COVERED

When we attempt to cover our own sins, we are like a little kid who spills an entire carton of milk and tries to cover it up with a paper towel. We can't cover our mess. But if we uncover it, if we come to God with our sin, He covers it for us.

3. DOES NOT CHARGE

God's grace is amazing. If we are His, He does not charge us with sin. Instead He charges or credits us with His righteousness and forgiveness. In our place, Jesus was charged with our sin so we could be credited with His perfection.

Of this passage, Martin Luther said something very powerful: "We are all sinners alike, only that the sins of the holy are not counted but covered; and the sins of the unholy are not covered but counted."[6]

You are no better than any other man. You have sinned as all men have sinned—including David. But Christ has covered your sins and not charged you with them. Rejoice in that reality today.

David's sins were awful—why would God choose to cover them and forgive him?

When was a time you felt God's forgiveness? Thank Him for it today.

FUTILITY!

ECCLESIASTES 1

Stonehenge has been a mystery for centuries. What is it? Who built it? Where did it come from? How did it end up in the English countryside? One theory is that the stones were moved there from a hill 150 miles away. To learn as much as possible about the source of the rocks, archaeologists have been digging on that hill for 90 years. But in 2013, geologists discovered that the archaeologists have been digging on the wrong hill. The hill they should have been excavating was a mile away. For 90 years, they centered their lives on the wrong hill.[7]

Imagine the misery of learning you have squandered so much time in pursuit of the wrong thing.

In the Book of Ecclesiastes, Solomon—David's son and the king the Lord gave wisdom to—wrote that everything in this life, everything under the sun, is absolutely futile. While Solomon walked with the Lord, the Lord gave him great insight, and we have much to learn from him.

Read Ecclesiastes 1 and take note of all that is described as futile. Underline them in your Bible or write them in the margins here.

When did you spend a lot of time on something, only for it to end up pointless? Maybe it was busy work at school or a task at your job. How did it make you feel for all of your work to be for nothing?

We see the futility of trying to accomplish things. Though the streams outlast us, they can never fill the sea—no matter how hard they work. In other words, any work we do "under the sun" is totally futile (v. 7).

We see the futility of seeking pleasure. No matter how many movies, apps, websites, games, albums, or TV shows we have, the eye and the ear remain unsatisfied. Vacations end. Trophies fade. Pleasures never last. They are futile, too (v. 8).

OK, well, if working for accomplishments and seeking pleasure are empty, what about working to leave behind a legacy? Futile. Generations from now, no one will remember you (v. 11).

We even see the futility of laboring in blessing. Solomon tried to find joy in the blessing the Lord gave him—his wisdom. But that too is folly and "a pursuit of the wind" (v. 17). Laboring for accomplishment, pleasure, and legacy is futile. Even laboring and finding identity in the blessings of God is futility.

I'm sure you're thinking, *Alright, enough, this is getting pretty depressing.* But it's important for us to understand the pain of a broken and fallen world, so we can know there is hope.

The word futile is used 38 times throughout the Book of Ecclesiastes—but it's used only once in the New Testament. The apostle Paul explained why this life is filled with futility in Romans 8:20. He wrote:

> *For the creation was subjected to futility—not willingly, but because of him who subjected it—in hope that the creation itself will also be set free from the bondage to decay into the glorious freedom of God's children.*
> **ROMANS 8:20**

Think back to Genesis. Before sin entered the world, everything was perfect. Nothing was futile. But humanity sinned and everything humankind was responsible for suffered. Creation was subjected to futility because God judged creation as a result of our sin. But He also gave creation hope that there will be a day when all things will be made new. When Christ returns, He will rescue all of creation from futility.

Creation will one day be rescued from futility, and the same One who will rescue all of creation can rescue us from futility now. You don't have to be a man who lives under the sun. You don't have to live only for this world. You don't have to chip away at the wrong hill. We can rest in the One who came here for us—the One who did all the work for us on the cross, Jesus, who gives us rest from futility in this life. Only the King of kings can rescue us from the futility of futilities.

What is the opposite of futile?

If everything is futile, then what's the point of prayer?

How do you get caught up in running after things that are futile? How can you focus instead on things that are lasting?

GET WISDOM

PROVERBS

When Solomon became king, he asked the Lord for wisdom. God graciously responded:

> *Since this was in your heart, and you have not requested riches, wealth, or glory, or for the life of those who hate you, and you have not even requested long life, but you have requested for yourself wisdom and knowledge that you may judge my people over whom I have made you king, wisdom and knowledge are given to you. I will also give you riches, wealth, and glory, unlike what was given to the kings who were before you, or will be given to those after you.*
> **2 CHRONICLES 1:11-12**

Solomon is the major writer in the Book of Proverbs. Proverbs is a great manual for how to be a man of God, full of sayings fathers and sons alike can use to find wisdom. It's unlike any other book in the Bible, full of extremely practical advice we can use every day. It's like a written account of every wise thing your mom and dad ever said, or an index of FAQ's for how to grow as a man of God.

Reflect on these questions and proverbs today:

How important is wisdom?

> *Wisdom is supreme—so get wisdom. And whatever else you get, get understanding. Cherish her, and she will exalt you; if you embrace her, she will honor you.*
> **PROVERBS 4:7-8**

Where does wisdom come from?

> *The fear of the LORD is the beginning of knowledge; fools despise wisdom and discipline.*
> **PROVERBS 1:7**

What is most important to look for in a woman?

Charm is deceptive and beauty is fleeting, but a woman who fears the LORD will be praised.
PROVERBS 31:30

Should I do what the culture/world advises?

There is a way that seems right to a person, but its end is the way to death.
PROVERBS 14:12

Do I need community as a man?

Iron sharpens iron, and one person sharpens another.
PROVERBS 27:17

What happens to the proud?

Pride comes before destruction, and an arrogant spirit before a fall.
PROVERBS 16:18

How should I speak to people?

A gentle answer turns away anger, but a harsh word stirs up wrath.
PROVERBS 15:1

Should I work hard?

Go to the ant, you slacker! Observe its ways and become wise. Without leader, administrator, or ruler, it prepares its provisions in summer; it gathers its food during harvest. How long will you stay in bed, you slacker? When will you get up from your sleep? A little sleep, a little slumber, a little folding of the arms to rest, and your poverty will come like a robber, your need, like a bandit.
PROVERBS 6:6-11

How should I view debt?

The rich rule over the poor, and the borrower is a slave to the lender.
PROVERBS 22:7

Does my reputation matter?

A good name is to be chosen over great wealth; favor is better than silver and gold.
PROVERBS 22:1

Do my close friends matter?

The one who walks with the wise will become wise, but a companion of fools will suffer harm.
PROVERBS 13:20

Do those who cannot defend themselves matter?

Speak up for those who have no voice, for the justice of all who are dispossessed. Speak up, judge righteously, and defend the cause of the oppressed and needy.
PROVERBS 31:8-9

What's the difference between wisdom and knowledge? Why should we seek wisdom?

Who is the wisest person you know? What makes them wise?

Where does the world look for wisdom? Why should we look to God's Word?

5

SEASON 5

EXILE & RETURN

MORE BROKEN PROMISES

| CREATION & FALL | 2000 BC PROMISE & A PEOPLE | 1400 BC RESCUE & LAW | 1000 BC LAND & KINGDOM | 600 BC EXILE & RETURN | AD JESUS | AD 30 A NEW PEOPLE | A BETTER BEGINNING |

We must be careful we don't mistake God's patience for apathy. He's patient with us—but He's not apathetic toward our sin. We see this in the story of Solomon: When God promises that He will discipline His people out of love, He makes good on it.

Here are three things we learn about God during this season.

1. GOD REBUKES

Read 1 Kings 11:1–8.

God's people worshiped Yahweh, while other groups worshiped their own little-g gods. As Solomon married women from other tribes, however, he invited them to build altars to their own gods. King Solomon—the son of David—allowed idolatry to enter his heart and cover the land. God had warned him: If you allow idolatry to cover the land, I will remove you from it. And that's what He did.

> *This disaster happened because the people of Israel sinned against the LORD their God who had brought them out of the land of Egypt from the power of Pharaoh king of Egypt and because they had worshiped other gods. They lived according to the customs of the nations that the LORD had dispossessed before the Israelites and according to what the kings of Israel did. The Israelites secretly did things against the Lord their God that were not right. They built high places in all their towns from watchtower to fortified city. They set up for themselves sacred pillars and Asherah poles on every high hill and under every green tree. They burned incense on all the high places just like those nations that the Lord had driven out before them had done. They did evil things, angering the LORD. They served idols, although the Lord had told them, "You must not do this." Still, the LORD warned Israel and Judah through every prophet and every seer, saying, "Turn from your evil ways and keep my commands and statutes according to whole law I commanded your ancestors and sent to you through my servants the prophets."*
> **2 KINGS 17:7-13**

On every hill and under every tree, God's people found something to worship other than Him. This was the promised land! It was a place God had given them after rescuing them from Egypt. God made good on His promise to discipline His people. And it all started when Solomon allowed his wives to build altars to their own gods.

What does it mean that God is patient with us, even in our sin?

When was a time you were disciplined for something you did? Do you think the punishment was fair? Why or why not?

Is God right to punish us when we sin? Explain.

2. GOD REMEMBERS

Even while God rebuked His people for their sin, He remembered His promises to them. He remembered the promise to Abraham, Isaac, and Jacob that they would be a people that would bless all nations. He remembered His promise to David that his kingdom would last forever. God remembers His promises.

But I will remember the covenant I made with you in the days of your youth, and I will establish a permanent covenant with you.
EZEKIEL 16:60

For I will take you from the nations and gather you from all the countries, and will bring you into your own land. I will also sprinkle clean water on you, and you will be clean. I will cleanse you from all your impurities and all your idols. I will give you a new heart and put a new spirit within you; I will remove your heart of stone and give you a heart of flesh. I will place my Spirit within you and cause you to follow my statutes and carefully observe my ordinances.
EZEKIEL 36:24-27

How does God use discipline for our good?

We see here what God promised Israel. What does God promise us today?

How is Jesus the fulfillment of God's promises?

3. GOD RESTORES

In the first year of King Cyrus of Persia, in order to fulfill the word of the Lord spoken through Jeremiah, the Lord roused the spirit of King Cyrus of Persia to issue a proclamation throughout his entire kingdom and also to put it in writing: This is what King Cyrus of Persia says: The Lord, the God of the heavens, has given me all the kingdoms of the earth and has appointed me to build him a temple at Jerusalem in Judah. Any of his people among you may go up, and may the Lord his God be with him.

2 CHRONICLES 36:22-23

The king of Persia allowed God's people to go back to their land, but when they went back, God's people saw it was in ruin. Walls had fallen. Houses were gone. Looking around, they knew the promise of an everlasting kingdom had to be more than what they saw around them. It had to be about something yet to come. The Old Testament ends hopelessly like this to show us we need a new heart. To show us our longing for Jesus, who would come and change everything.

How would you define the word "restore"? What does it mean in this context?

How is Jesus the ultimate restoration of God's promises?

SEASON 5

PERSONAL BIBLE STUDY

The passages you will study this week chronicle events that happened during the period of history we covered in the Season 5 group discussion. God's people were united under King David and enjoyed a season of peace and prosperity. But David's son, Solomon, compromised his devotion to God and pursued the gods of his wives and concubines. The nation spiraled down spiritually. God sent prophets to warn the people of coming judgment if they did not turn back, but the people did not heed the warnings. So just as God had promised, He removed His people from the land because of their idolatry. But God did not abandon them during their exile. As prophesied, God's people returned to their land. However, their hearts were still not fully committed to Him, thus the need for the coming Messiah.

DAY 1

PROVE IT

1 KINGS 18

"Oh yeah? Prove it."

When was the last time someone challenged you? Maybe it was in an argument or right before a race. It could have been during a game of one-on-one or H-O-R-S-E. It can be nerve-wracking having to prove yourself—there's no middle ground. Either you come off as the real deal or a fraud. You win or lose.

When someone tells you to prove it, there's no going back.

Read 1 Kings 18.

This is an incredible story that highlights the difference between God and the false gods that the people were tempted to worship. Elijah, a prophet of God, issued a challenge to 450 prophets of a false (little-g) god named Baal. Elijah issued the challenge: *Let's find out whose god is God. You pray to your god, Baal. I will pray to my God, Yahweh, the self-existing One. The god who answers by fire is really God. You guys go first.*

Prove it.

The 450 prophets of Baal danced around the fire for hours. They cut themselves, screamed, and begged their god to light the altar on fire. Baal, answer us!

Elijah threw down some ancient smack talk. *Shout a little louder,* he cried. *Maybe your god is sleeping. I wonder why he cannot hear you?* You can almost hear him laughing.

But there was no sound. No one answered. No one paid attention.

Then, Elijah stepped up and asked for water to be poured all over the altar, because He knew what was about to happen. He knew that his God hears, and his God answers. Elijah asked for the altar to be soaked so it would be clear that God is the One who sent the fire—no one could say it happened because two rocks rubbed together and created a spark or the sun caught a blade of grass on fire. He wanted it absolutely clear that God had answered. After Elijah prayed, fire came from heaven, consumed the altar, and licked up all the water on the ground.

Our God hears. Elijah wanted the people to understand how foolish it is to worship idols that cannot hear and gods that are powerless. Sadly, the people as a whole, even after this moment, continued to worship and pursue false gods rather than the one true God.

The things of this life we are tempted to pursue are powerless to save us, too. They are powerless to give us true life. God is the only One who can answer with fire.

What things of the world are you pursuing? How can you change your focus to pursue God?

How have you seen God do things in your life that only He could do?

What's keeping you from whole-heartedly pursuing Him now?

DAY 2

DIFFICULT CHOICES

DANIEL 3

Some people see living in America as living in a Christian nation, perhaps similar to the state of the nation of Israel during King David's reign. Under David's leadership, the people feared God and were united. But if you want to make a comparison between life as believers in the United States and life in the Old Testament for God's people, a more accurate comparison would be the period of Israel's Babylonian captivity. Like that time period, we are living in a time that is more and more secular and more and more tolerant of everything—of everything except people who insist that their belief system is absolute. So how should we live? Daniel's friends provide an example.

Daniel 3 tells the story of Shadrach, Meshach, and Abednego, though these were not their real names. The king of Babylon, Nebuchadnezzar, had besieged Jerusalem, taken the people into captivity, and given them new names and new jobs. Shadrach, Meshach, and Abednego tolerated the new jobs and new names, trusting God's plan for them in a new culture. But in Daniel 3, the king asked them to do something they were unwilling to do.

He announced that every person must bow down and worship a 90-foot gold statue that he had built. He set up an orchestra and told the people that as soon as the music started, they must bow down to worship the image. Anyone who did not worship the image would be cast into a fiery furnace.

When was a time recently you were faced with a difficult choice? What did you do?

The idols of this world aren't asking us to give up our worship of God, just to add them to the mix. But because God is the only true God, He says we must only worship Him.

Shadrach, Meshach, and Abednego refused to bow. King Nebuchadnezzar was furious, scolded them, and offered them another chance. They let him know that they, of course, did not need a second opportunity. They believed that God was able to rescue them, but if He chose not to, they still would not bow. So Nebuchadnezzar threw them into the furnace, a furnace so hot that it killed the soldiers who threw them in.

Read Daniel 3:24-30. What word would you use to describe the king's reaction once he saw what was happening?

Was it Christ who jumped in the fire with them? We're not sure—theologians have debated whether this was Christ or an angel. Regardless, after the guys walked out of the furnace, Nebuchadnezzar admitted, "There is no other god who is able to deliver like this" (Dan. 3:29).

In the pagan Babylonian culture, Shadrach, Meshach, and Abednego were willing to work new jobs and take new names. But they were not willing to bow to another god.

When the prophet Jeremiah wrote to God's people living in Babylon, he instructed them to build houses, plant gardens, live, and to even pray for the welfare of Babylon (Jer. 29:4-7). So living in Babylon, based on God's instructions, meant caring for people there and seeking the welfare of the city. But it also meant not compromising their commitment to God.

God put you in your school, your team, your clubs, your family, and your neighborhood on purpose. Live there. Pray for the people God has surrounded you with. Work hard. Do all you can for the welfare of those around you. As you do so, you'll be faced with difficult choices. That's part of being a man.

Don't give in. Only bow to Him.

Who can you turn to if you have to make a difficult decision?

When was a time you made a wise decision and were rewarded? How did it feel?

GOD IN THE STORY OF ESTHER

ESTHER

A king's heart is like channeled of water in the LORD's hand; He directs it wherever he chooses.
PROVERBS 21:1

The Book of Esther does not mention God by name. But since God is the center of the Bible story, how can there be a book that does not mention His name? In Esther, we learn that we must not mistake God's silence for His absence. Often He is working behind the scenes, directing events and implementing His plans.

Esther occurs after God's people have been taken into Babylonian captivity. The Persians conquered the Babylonians and set the Jews free to return home. But many stayed, continuing to live in a land that was not their own, under the rule of a Persian king. Esther opens with a massive feast held by the Persian king Xerxes, during which he decided to show off his wife, Vashti. He sent for her to come wearing her crown, but she refused. The king was livid, so he banned Vashti from his presence and launched a search throughout the royal provinces for a new queen.

Mordecai and his beautiful cousin Esther lived in one of the provinces. When Esther's parents died, Mordecai adopted her as his own daughter. During the search for a queen, she was taken into Xerxes' harem where other virgins were preparing to go before the king. Each day, Mordecai walked by the court where Esther stayed and talked with her. He encouraged her to conceal her nationality and family background as she hoped to be the next queen of Persia. Eventually Esther was summoned before the king, and he was blown away by her beauty. He loved her more than any of the others and made her his queen.

After Esther became queen, Mordecai happened to overhear a plot to assassinate the king. Mordecai told Esther who then told Xerxes, giving due credit to Mordecai. Mordecai had saved the king, but his reward was overlooked.

At this point in the story, a new character is introduced: Haman. He was promoted to a high position, right at the place in the story where we would expect to find a report of Mordecai's promotion. This seems incredibly unfair. Why wouldn't Mordecai get the credit? All the officials bowed down and paid honor to Haman except Mordecai. This infuriated Haman, and he devised a plan to destroy not only Mordecai, but all the Jews.

When was a time you felt you were overlooked for something you deserved? What was your reaction?

Esther had been queen for five years when Haman reported to the king that a certain ethnic group (the Jews) did not obey the king's laws and that they should be eliminated. Xerxes gave Haman full authority to do as he pleased, and Haman moved forward with his plan. By the end of the year, all the Jews would be annihilated.

When Mordecai heard the news, he mourned in sackcloth and ashes. After Esther tried to get him to cease his mourning, Mordecai sent word to her about what was happening, with a command for her to go to the king. This frightened Esther. But Mordecai told her that she would face death regardless, and that perhaps she had been placed in this position "for such a time as this" (Esth. 4:14). To save her people, Esther had to risk her life before the king and before Haman. When she walked into the king's presence, he accepted her and offered her anything she wanted up to half the kingdom. She simply asked for he and Haman to attend a banquet. In the meantime, Haman had built massive gallows on which to hang Mordecai because he still refused to bow before Haman.

When Esther told the king that she and her people were to be killed, Xerxes' honor was offended that someone would make such plans and he walked out of the room in a rage. The gallows Haman had built for Mordecai were used on Haman. And because Haman was executed as a traitor, his property was confiscated and given to Esther. The king's signet ring which had previously been given to Haman was given to Mordecai. The ring vested Mordecai with the power and authority previously given to Haman. Esther and Mordecai wrote a decree that Jews could take whatever measures were necessary to defend themselves. In the armed conflict, the Jews struck down those who hated them. They were victorious.

This fight was the foundation of a Jewish holiday, one that exists to this day, Purim. Passover celebrates the deliverance of the Jews through extraordinary events. Purim celebrates the survival of the Jews through ordinary events.

The author of Esther was teaching God's people that sometimes God quietly works behind the scenes for their benefit. The Passover remembers a time when God delivered His people from Egyptian captivity through very visible and awe-inspiring miracles such as the plagues. In Esther, God is the silent yet sovereign King, orchestrating events and working behind the scenes to rescue His people.

God is working in the ordinary details of your life, too. He is still the sovereign King using great and small things to accomplish His purposes.

How have you seen God work behind the scenes in your ordinary life?

When was a time you felt like you weren't hearing from God?

How did you pray during this time? What did you learn?

WORSHIP IN DUTY OR DELIGHT

MALACHI 1–3

Malachi was a messenger to God's people after they returned from Babylonian exile. However, while the people had returned and were worshiping God again, their worship was out of duty rather than delight. The priests were offering God leftover animals and not bringing their best to Him.

Read Malachi 1:6-14.

> **Does church ever feel like something you have to do? List three words to describe how you think God wants us to view church.**

According to Leviticus 22, priests were to only bring pure and unblemished animals to sacrifice to God. But now, the priests were offering God blind and diseased animals. God essentially said that their boss (their governor) would fire them if they had offered him what they were offering God. God preferred no offering in comparison to a half-hearted, going-through-the-motions type of offering.

> **Have you ever received a gift that you knew was half-hearted? What was your reaction?**

Some struggle with God's insistence on being worshiped, as if this makes God like the insecure guy at school who constantly wants attention. But the guy at school acts that way because he is deficient in his character. There is nothing deficient in God's character. He passionately pursues His own worship because there is nothing greater for Him to pursue. Here are three thoughts to consider:

1. GOD MUST BE WORSHIPED

Notice Malachi 1:11. God's name will be great among the nations. God was declaring that He would find worshipers from every nation. And He does. Christ was sacrificed to rescue people from every tribe, tongue, and nation. He pursues worshipers from outside of Israel—including you. He is always worshiped—always. When you sleep at night, someone on the other side of the world is worshiping. If God did not desire and demand worship, He would not be God. If there were something more excellent, more beautiful, and more praiseworthy than God, then that thing would be God. But there is nothing better, nothing more amazing than Him. He stands alone.

2. WE WILL WORSHIP

The people God was addressing hadn't stopped worshiping; they had just stopped worshiping Him. They viewed something else as greater than God. You don't have to be taught to worship. You are always giving value and worth to something or someone. But God alone is Master and Father, and anything else we worship is less than Him.

Are you worshiping anything in your life other than God? Why?

3. THUS, HIS COMMANDS TO WORSHIP HIM ARE GRACIOUS INVITATIONS

These words in Malachi are very strong. But when we understand that God must be worshiped and we must worship, we realize that God pursuing our worship is good for us. His commands to worship Him are gracious invitations because He is commanding us to find ultimate joy.

The Old Testament ends during this period of time. Nehemiah rebuilt the wall, but the people could not keep their commitments. The exiles were back in the land, but were now offering God leftover sacrifices. While some have been faithful, the overarching trend of God's people was a failure to worship God alone. They needed a Rescuer. So do we. Malachi prophesied that the Rescuer is coming.

> See, I am going to send my messenger, and he will clear the way before me. Then the Lord you seek will suddenly come to his temple, the Messenger of the covenant you delight in—see, he is coming," says the Lord of Armies.
> **MALACHI 3:1**

The messenger who clears the way will be John the Baptist. Christ is the Messenger of the new covenant—a new promise that will include people from every nation. He is also the mediator of the new covenant as He brings us to Himself through His death on the cross. The Old Testament ends with people desperate for the One who will change our disobedient hearts. The Old Testament ends with a longing for a new King, a better King.

Think back over all the stories we've read from the Old Testament. How does the overarching narrative point toward Christ?

What is one way you can worship God out of delight this week?

6

JESUS

THE STORY IS FULFILLED

CREATION & FALL	PROMISE & A PEOPLE	RESCUE & LAW	LAND & KINGDOM	EXILE & RETURN	JESUS	A NEW PEOPLE	A BETTER BEGINNING
	2000 BC	1400 BC	1000 BC	600 BC	AD	AD 30	

If you look back at the timeline, you can see how everything we've looked at so far points to Jesus. In Season 1, our hearts are broken and we rebel. In Season 2, God makes a promise to His people and Abraham laughs in return. In Season 3, God rescues His people from Egyptian slavery and they choose to worship golden calves. In Season 4, God delivers His people into the promised land and they continue to worship things other than Him. In Season 5, He sends His people into captivity and then He brings them back. Throughout the Old Testament, we see how our hearts are unable to obey Him. We need our hearts to be rescued. We need our hearts to be changed. This is why Jesus comes.

As the New Testament begins, God's people are longing for a King who will rescue them and change their hearts. Here is how the four gospels present Jesus as the answer to this longing:

1. THE KING HAS ARRIVED

The beginning of the gospel of Jesus Christ, the Son of God. As it is written in Isaiah the prophet … In those days Jesus came from Nazareth in Galilee and was baptized in the Jordan by John. As soon as he came up out of the water, he saw the heavens being torn open and the Spirit descending on him like a dove. And a voice came from heaven: "You are my beloved Son; with you I am well-pleased."
MARK 1:1-2,9-11

An account of the genealogy of Jesus Christ, the Son of David, the Son of Abraham:
MATTHEW 1:1

… son of Enos, son of Seth, son of Adam, son of God
LUKE 3:38

In the beginning was the Word, and the Word was with God, and the Word was God. He was with God in the beginning. All things were created through him, and apart from Him not one thing was created that has been created.
JOHN 1:1-3

God's people crossed the Jordan to enter the promised land—the same river where Jesus was baptized. What is the significance?

Matthew points to David and Abraham, Luke points to Adam, and John points to the beginning of creation. Why is it important that we trace Jesus back into the Old Testament?

2. HIS KINGDOM IS ANNOUNCED

After John was arrested, Jesus went to Galilee, proclaiming the good news of God: "The time is fulfilled, and the kingdom of God has come near. Repent and believe in the good news!"
MARK 1:14-15

Then John's disciples told him about all these things. So John summoned two of his disciples and sent them to the Lord, asking, "Are you the one who is to come, or should we expect someone else?" When the men reached him, they said, "John the Baptist sent us to ask you, 'Are you the one who is to come, or should we expect someone else?'" At that time Jesus healed many people of diseases, afflictions, and evil spirits, and he granted sight to many blind people. He replied to them, "Go and report to John what you have seen and heard: The blind receive their sight, the lame walk, those with leprosy are cleansed, the deaf hear, the dead are raised, and the poor are told the good news,
LUKE 7:18-22

3. HIS KINGDOM IS UPSIDE-DOWN

Jesus went up the mountain and summoned those he wanted, and they came to him. He appointed twelve, whom he also named them apostles, to be with him, to send them out to preach.
MARK 3:13-14

The Son of Man came eating and drinking, and they say, "Look, a glutton and a drunkard, a friend of tax collectors and sinners!"
MATTHEW 11:19A

"Truly I tell you," he said, "unless you turn and become like children, you will never enter the kingdom of heaven."
MATTHEW 18:3

Why is it important to us that Jesus is a friend to sinners?

Why does Jesus say that we have to be like children to enter the kingdom? What implications does this have on us as men?

4. THE KING SERVES AND SUFFERS

When they approached Jerusalem and came to Bethphage at the Mount of Olives, Jesus then sent two disciples, telling them, "Go into the village ahead of you. At once you will find a donkey tied there with her foal. Untie them and bring them to me. If anyone says anything to you, say that the Lord needs them, and he will send them at once." This took place so that what was spoken through the prophet might be fulfilled: Tell Daughter Zion, "See, your King is coming to you, gentle, and mounted on a donkey, and on a colt, the foal of donkey."
MATTHEW 21:1-5

After crucifying him, they divided his clothes by casting lots. Then they sat down and were guarding him there. Above his head they put up the charge against him in writing: THIS IS JESUS, THE KING OF THE JEWS.
MATTHEW 27:35-37

Why did Jesus enter Jerusalem on a donkey?

The soldiers were mocking Jesus by calling Him the King of the Jews. If He really were a king, he would be on a throne—not dying on a cross. What kind of a king is Jesus?

5. THE KING CONQUERS

Then He took the Twelve aside and told them, "See, we are going up to Jerusalem. Everything that is written through the prophets about the Son of Man will be accomplished. For he will be handed over to the Gentiles, and he will be mocked, insulted, spit on; and after they flog him, they will kill him, and he will rise on the third day.
LUKE 18:31-33

Everything we've looked at so far in the Bible points to Jesus.

1. Jesus is greater than <u>Adam.</u>

2. Jesus is greater than <u>Abraham.</u>

3. Jesus is greater than <u>Moses.</u>

4. Jesus is greater than <u>David.</u>

5. Jesus is greater than <u>the prophets.</u>

How is your view of the Old Testament different following the arrival of Jesus?

Why is it important that we see Jesus' death through the lens of the Old Testament?

SEASON 6

PERSONAL BIBLE STUDY

Our Season 6 group discussion focused on Jesus, the King who has come to serve and save. We discussed how His kingdom is not like an earthly kingdom, but is totally turned upside down. We also reinforced the truth that all of Scripture points to Jesus. The story is about Him. In your personal study this week, you'll examine an account of Jesus making that point Himself. You'll also learn more about Jesus' kingdom and who is fit for it.

DAY 1

THE FIRST EASTER SERMON

LUKE 24

When we think of Jesus' resurrection, we often think that's the end of His story. But the beauty is that it isn't. Not only did Jesus conquer the grave, but immediately after He began to do what He did best: He pursued people, to ensure they understood the reality of His resurrection.

His first message was heard by two guys who were walking the seven miles from Jerusalem to Emmaus. As Jesus began walking along with them, He asked what they were talking about. One of the men, Cleopas, responded with a hint of sarcasm: "Are you the only visitor in Jerusalem who doesn't know ... ?" (Luke 24:18). They then shared the news that Jesus of Nazareth, who had performed miracles, wowed crowds, and spoken with incredible authority, had been crucified. They were deeply disappointed because they had hoped Jesus was the one to rescue Israel. They were also troubled by reports that angels were declaring Jesus was alive. It was a lot to process. Jesus rebuked them for their weak faith.

> *He said to them, "How foolish and slow you are to believe all that the prophets spoken! Wasn't it necessary for the Messiah to suffer these things and enter into his glory?" Then beginning with Moses and all the Prophets, he interpreted for them the things concerning himself in all the Scriptures.*
> **LUKE 24:25-27**

Do you ever have a difficult time believing God's promises? How do you think Jesus would respond to your doubt?

Jesus then showed them how all the Scripture points to Him. (Sound familiar?) They didn't recognize Him until after He had blessed, broken, and given them bread. Jesus then disappeared. The two men hurried back to Jerusalem to find the disciples. As they were sharing how Jesus found them on the road and preached His own Easter sermon, Jesus appeared to the whole group. He showed them His hands and feet.

He told them, "These are my words that I spoke to you while I was still with you—that everything written about me in the Law of Moses, the Prophets, and the Psalms must be fulfilled." Then he opened their minds to understand the Scriptures. He also said to them, "This is what is written: The Messiah would suffer and rise from the dead the third day, and repentance for forgiveness of sins would be proclaimed in his name to all the nations, beginning at Jerusalem."
LUKE 24:44-47

For the Jews, their entire Bible was the Law, the Prophets, and the Psalms. Therefore, Jesus was essentially saying, "All that you have read and studied points to Me." In the Law, God gave His people commands and set up a priest and sacrificial system because of man's inability to keep the commands. In the Prophets, God spoke through men to call His people to truth, justice, and faithfulness. In Psalms, God's people celebrated the rule of God. Many of the psalms were written by David, the king who, though deeply flawed, united the people and ruled them skillfully. Because Jesus is the point of all the Scripture, we see that He is the perfect Priest, the perfect Prophet, and the perfect King.

> **Why is it significant that it took Jesus breaking bread with the men for them to recognize Him?**

> **Have you ever felt God "open your mind" to understand Him? What was it like?**

1. JESUS IS THE PERFECT PRIEST (THE LAW)

While priests in the Old Testament needed to offer sacrifices every single day, Jesus offered Himself for our sins "once for all" (Heb. 7:27). On the cross He yelled out, "It is finished" (John 19:30) because the full payment for our sins was paid, and the wrath of God was quenched. Other priests offered animals as sacrifices, but Christ offered Himself as the pure and perfect sacrifice—the sacrifice to end all other sacrifices.

> **What does it mean for your daily life that Jesus is your Priest?**

2. JESUS IS THE PERFECT PROPHET (THE PROPHETS)

The prophets confronted people in their sin and called the people to repentance. Jesus likewise called people to repentance, but also called them to Himself. "Repent" and "Come to Me" were messages He heralded. Jesus is full of both truth and grace. He is also the Prophet to whom all other prophets pointed.

> **In the Old Testament, prophets called people to repentance. What does God use today to accomplish the same thing? What role does Jesus play?**

3. JESUS IS THE PERFECT KING (THE PSALMS)

Every other king, even the good ones, fell woefully short of God's greatness and grace. He stands alone as the King of kings. King David wrote of the Faithful One who would not see decay in Psalm 16:

> *Therefore my heart is glad and my whole being rejoices; my body also rests securely. For you will not abandon me to Sheol; you will not allow your faithful one to see decay.*
> **PSALM 16:9-10**

Clearly David was not speaking of himself, because David's body did see decay. But King Jesus' body never did. Not only did He preach His own Easter sermon, He rose from the grave before He did. He is the King who rules and reigns forever. Jesus is your perfect Priest, Prophet, and King.

> **How does it change your view of the gospel to think of Jesus as an eternal, perfect King?**

THE BIRDS OF THE SKY

MATTHEW 13:31-32

As we talked about in our group session, Jesus announced the good news of His kingdom. He is the King who rules and reigns forever, and we are invited into His kingdom.

Jesus also taught about the kingdom of heaven through parables. In Matthew 13, He offered six parables about His kingdom. Let's look at one of those parables today:

> He presented another parable to them: "The kingdom of heaven is like a mustard seed that a man took and sowed in his field. It's the smallest of all the seeds, but when grown, it's taller than the garden plants and becomes a tree, so that the birds of the sky come and nest in its branches."
> **MATTHEW 13:31-32**

When Jesus said the kingdom of heaven is like a tiny mustard seed, perhaps the crowd understood that He meant the kingdom of heaven on this earth would start small. And it did. For the most part, Christ's arrival on earth was unnoticed by the vast majority of humanity. It wasn't tweeted about. No one live streamed it. It wasn't covered by the news channel.

On the night of Christ's birth, no one even provided Joseph and Mary a room. So Jesus was placed in a manger, a feeding trough for livestock. After His birth, He grew up in a backwoods town in Galilee, far from the influence and affluence of the Roman Empire. When Jesus was around 30, He began teaching publicly and performing miracles. He invited 12 disciples to live with Him and follow Him. These 12 disciples were normal guys, uneducated, not from the religious elite, rough around the edges, and impulsive. After Jesus died, rose from the dead, and ascended back to heaven, about 120 people gathered together in prayer in Jerusalem waiting for direction from the Holy Spirit on what to do next.

The kingdom of heaven started small.

Have you ever seen something small get bigger and bigger? Maybe someone you know posted a video that went viral or a campaign at school got really popular. What do you think causes some things to get so big so fast?

Jesus, however, assured His disciples the kingdom would not stay small. It would grow and become like a tree. In Israel, the mustard plant grew from an almost invisible seed to be as tall as 15 feet high. Like the mustard plant, the kingdom of heaven in this world has grown exponentially. The rule of God has expanded to people all over the globe. The kingdom is still expanding, in fact, and will continue to expand, including people from every tribe, tongue, and nation.

Even as you are doing this study with a group of guys, there are millions of other men around the world studying the Bible. Some do so in secret because it is illegal to be a Christian and their lives are in constant danger. Some are meeting under trees in remote villages because they have nowhere indoors to go. But today, in many different languages and dialects, Christ is being praised and glorified and the kingdom of heaven is expanding. What Jesus said would happen has happened and continues to happen.

But that is not all Jesus was saying in this parable. The kingdom grows to a large tree "so that the birds of the sky come and nest in its branches" (v. 32). What does He mean by this?

This phrase took the listeners back to several Old Testament passages describing earthly kingdoms that were so powerful and fruitful that people outside of those kingdoms benefited from them. When Israel was in Babylonian captivity under Nebuchadnezzar, Daniel interpreted the ruler's dream. In Nebuchadnezzar's dream, he saw the following:

> The tree grew large and strong; its top reached to the sky, and it was visible to the ends of the earth. Its leaves were beautiful, its fruit was abundant, and on it was food for all. Wild animals found shelter under it, the birds of the sky lived in its branches, and every creature was fed from it.
> **DANIEL 4:11-12**

Daniel told the king of Babylon, "That tree is you" (Dan. 4:22). The Babylonian kingdom was so fruitful that it influenced the culture, education, architecture, and philosophy of other nations.

The crowd also knew of the Assyrian kingdom. When the Assyrian kingdom was prospering, the "birds of the sky nested in its branches" (Ezek. 31:6). Both Babylonian and Assyrian kingdoms impacted outsiders.

And so it is with the kingdom of heaven. The kingdom of heaven influences people outside of the kingdom. If you are a Christian, people at your school and in your neighborhood benefit from your influence. As you walk with integrity, work hard, love and forgive people, and bring your best every day, you bless and influence others. You are a part of a people that blesses all other peoples. And as we influence the world around us, we are commanded to invite others into His kingdom. We are commanded to make disciples, urging others to receive His forgiveness and to live with Jesus as their King.

While the Babylonian, Assyrian, and other kingdoms rose and fell, the kingdom of heaven will never end. Our King reigns forever and ever.

How are you influencing people outside the kingdom of heaven? What skills and abilities do you have that God can use?

THE PHARISEE AND THE TAX COLLECTOR

LUKE 18:9-14

The people who are fit for the kingdom of God, the kingdom that Jesus inaugurated, are not the strong, the proud, or the type of people you might expect. To enter His kingdom, we must become humble like children. In other words, in order to enter His kingdom, we must embrace our weaknesses and realize how desperately we need Him.

Jesus told a parable about a Pharisee and a tax collector. One was qualified for His kingdom and the other was not. But the story had a twist ending. Jesus shocked the crowd when He revealed who was justified and right with God.

Pharisees were religious and devout individuals. The word Pharisee means "the separated ones," stemming from their desire to live lives that were holy and pure. They fasted twice a week. They tithed. They prayed regularly. They did everything imaginable to show they were serious about their faith. Moms wanted their kids to be Pharisees.

Tax collectors were the complete opposite. They were known as traitors because they worked for Rome, the foreign invaders who occupied the land. They were also seen as thieves, hiking up rates to line their own pockets. They were despised.

So when Jesus wanted to make a point to the religious people about not trusting in their own works, He told a story about a Pharisee and a tax collector.

We often think about humanity in terms of good people and bad people. If a story's main characters are a Pharisee and a tax collector, we think, then this story is going to be about a good, religious man and a bad, sinful one. But Jesus looks at humanity differently. All of us have sinned. "There is no one righteous, no even one" (Rom. 3:10).

He views us in terms of humble and proud.

Read Luke 18:9-14.

The Pharisee celebrated his own goodness. Even though he addressed God, he really prayed to himself about himself. He listed all the things that he was not. *I am so glad I am not greedy. I am not unrighteous. I am not an adulterer like other people I know. And I am not like this tax collector who steals money from others.* He then listed some of the things he did. *I fast. I give. And look at me right now, I am praying.* Yet for all that activity, this Pharisee never really encountered the Lord. Because when we encounter the Lord, we declare how great He is, not how great we are.

Do you know someone who goes out of their way to show off? Maybe it's someone who wants everyone to know they're the best student, or first chair in band, or the best on the team. How would God rather us act?

The Pharisee looked down on others because of his pride in all he was doing for God. Anytime we think we are righteous in our own goodness, we will immediately look down on others. We will consider ourselves a special kind of Christian, at a level to which others have not arrived. But we can't bring our spiritual résumé to Christ in pride. If we attempt to stand before Him in our own goodness, we insult Him, saying we believe His death was in vain.

The tax collector's prayer was very different from the Pharisee's. The tax collector mourned his own sinfulness. He would not even look up to heaven. He prayed, "God, have mercy on me, a sinner" (v. 13). The language here is powerful. When he begged God for mercy, he used the word *hilaskomai*, which is translated *propitiation*. It is a powerful word that is used several times in the New Testament. It is the same word used to describe the mercy seat on top of the Ark of the Covenant.

Remember that the scene for Jesus' parable is the temple. Inside the temple was the Most Holy Place where the high priest would enter once a year to make atonement for the sins of the people. Before entering, the high priest would take a goat and sacrifice it on the altar in the outer court of the temple. He would take the blood from the goat and bring it into the Most Holy Place, then sprinkle it on the seat of propitiation, also called the mercy seat, which served as the lid of the Ark of the Covenant. Inside the Ark of the Covenant were the Ten Commandments, the commandments that bring condemnation because we are unable to live up to them. The blood being sprinkled on the seat of propitiation signified that God's wrath was being appeased. It was turned from His people and placed instead on the goat that was sacrificed. The goat received the punishment instead of the people.

In Jesus' story, the tax collector understands this truth. He is outside the temple, hearing the sacrifices being made and saying, "God, let those sacrifices bear the punishment for my sin. I know that because You are holy, You can't just forget my sin. It has to be punished. Please God, turn Your wrath for my sin away from me."

The tax collector mourned his own sinfulness, and he went home justified.

Look up the definition of the word *justified*. Write it down in your Bible or in the margins here.

The word *justified* means he went home in complete right standing with God. The tax collector did not merely go home with his sins forgotten; he went home right with God. He went home with the perfection of God applied to his life. He went home as if he had never stolen, never lied, never cheated, always done the right thing, always treated people the right way, always been loving and gracious. He went home as if he had obeyed every commandment his whole life. He went home right with God not because he, in his own merit, actually lived those commandments, but because God had justified him.

Men who are justified are men who realize they are weak before God, in need of His mercy and grace, and call out to Him in faith. Men who are like the Pharisee are prideful and full of themselves. In reality, they are men who are really empty.

How does the world want you to act as a man? How does this line up or go against how God wants you to act?

What does it mean to "find strength in our weakness"? How do we make ourselves weak before God?

MIRACLE OF BREAD

JOHN 6

The miracles Jesus performed proved He is the eternal King. When John the Baptist sent people to ask Jesus if He was the One, Jesus sent word back that the sick are healed, the dead raised, and the blind receive sight. The miracles supported His claims to deity. The only miracle recorded in all four Gospel accounts, however, is the miracle of Jesus feeding 5,000 men. (We often say "feeding the 5,000," but when you include women and children, the crowd would have been much larger.)

Read John 6:1-14 and John 6:22-35.

Jesus made several famous "I AM" statements in the Gospel of John. His declaration "I am the bread of life" was the first (v. 35).

When Jesus declared to be "I AM," He was declaring to be God. As we learned earlier, long before Jesus walked the earth, God spoke to Moses from a burning bush, calling him to lead God's people out of Egyptian slavery to freedom. When Moses asked God what His name was, God replied, "I AM WHO I AM" (Ex. 3:14). So when Jesus referred to Himself as I AM, He was declaring to be the One who spoke to Moses from the bush, the One who is from the beginning, the One who is God.

Later in the Gospel of John, Jesus shocked and infuriated the crowd by saying, "Before Abraham was, I am" (John 8:58). He was declaring His eternal nature—that He was before Abraham, and that He has always been. The crowd attempted to stone Him to death because they viewed His statement as blasphemy, and the punishment for blasphemy was death. Jesus was either guilty of blasphemy, or He is indeed God.

Why is it important that Jesus existed both in the New Testament and in the time of Moses and Abraham? Is this hard for you to make sense of?

Of course, anyone can claim to be God. You may have a friend who talks a big game on the court, or a cousin who is always one-upping you with some story about something great he pulled off. Anyone can claim anything. But Jesus did much more than just claim to be God. He backed it up.

When Jesus declared, "I am the resurrection and the life," He raised Lazarus from the dead (John 11:25). When Jesus declared, "I am the light of the world," He put light into a blind man's eyes (John 9:5). And before Jesus declared, "I am the bread of life," He fed 5,000 men with two fish and five bread loaves (John 6:35). No one but Jesus can pull that off.

The crowd knew the story of Moses and the "bread from heaven": After their ancestors were freed from Egypt, they wandered in the desert before entering the promised land. During that time, God fed His people by providing manna from heaven.

Jesus told the crowd that in Him, God was now giving them the true bread from heaven. Jesus is better. He is the eternal bread from heaven, the One who came to sustain us and satisfy our souls. When we receive Him, when we feast on Him, we are never hungry again (John 6:35). Your grades, your girlfriend, your college choice, or your dream job—nothing will quench you. Only Jesus can. Only He is the Bread of life.

What is the connection between the manna from heaven and Jesus? How does the Old Testament point toward Him?

When was the last time you felt you were depending on Jesus?

What is holding you back from doing that today?

7

SEASON 7

A NEW PEOPLE

GOD'S MOBILE
HOME

	2000 BC	1400 BC	1000 BC	600 BC	AD	AD 30	
CREATION & FALL	PROMISE & A PEOPLE	RESCUE & LAW	LAND & KINGDOM	EXILE & RETURN	JESUS	A NEW PEOPLE	A BETTER BEGINNING

After the coming of Jesus, God's kingdom became an "already, but not yet" kingdom—it's already here because of Christ, but it's not yet totally fulfilled by His return. We live in the middle of that already/not yet. So what are the implications on our lives?

Let's look at what Jesus said right before His ascension into heaven in Acts:

> So when they had come together, they asked him, "Lord, are you restoring the kingdom to Israel at this time?" He said to them, "It is not for you to know times or periods that the Father has set by his own authority. But you will receive power when the Holy Spirit has come on you, and you will be my witnesses in Jerusalem, in all Judea and Samaria, and to the end of the earth."
> **ACTS 1:6-8**

The disciples want to know when Jesus is coming back, and His response is to send them out: In Jerusalem, He says, the Holy Spirit will descend upon them, and it is then up to them to be His disciples on earth in the interim.

This has massive implications on our lives. The Holy Spirit makes us new people, filled with God's presence and charged with the holy mission of spreading the gospel.

If someone asked you what the Holy Spirit is, what would you say?

If Jesus came, why do you think there is still so much brokenness in the world?

Why do you think Jesus did not tell His disciples when He was going to return?

Here are three thoughts about what it means to be a new people.

WE ARE ...
1. A NEW PEOPLE

For those of you who were baptized into Christ have been clothed with Christ. There is no Jew or Greek, slave or free, male or female; since you are all one in Christ Jesus. And if you belong to Christ, then you are Abraham's seed, heirs according to the promise.
GALATIANS 3:27-29

If you are a Christian, you have put on Christ like a garment. What does that mean? It means you are allowed to stand before God clothed in His righteousness—not your own.

How would you define the word "righteousness"?

Why are we allowed to wear Christ's righteousness before God?

2. WITH NEW POWER

So then you are no longer foreigners and strangers, but fellow citizens with the saints, and members of God's household, built on the foundation of the apostles and prophets, with Christ Jesus himself as the cornerstone. In him the whole building, being put together, grows into a holy temple in the Lord. In him you are also being built together for God's dwelling in the Spirit.
EPHESIANS 2:19-22

You don't put a cornerstone in at the end of a building—you lay the cornerstone first and the rest of the building is built around it. Jesus is our cornerstone because He is the center of our lives. The Christian faith demands that we die to our old lives and make Jesus the center around which everything else revolves.

If God lives in you, then wherever you go, you're a "holy sanctuary." How does knowing that change the way you act?

What would it look like for the different parts of your life (your school, your sports, your activities, etc.) to revolve around Christ?

3. ON A HOLY MISSION

Then Jesus came near and said to them, "All authority has been given to me in heaven and on earth. Go, therefore, and make disciples of all nations, baptizing them in the name of the Father and of the Son and of the Holy Spirit, teaching them to observe everything I have commanded you. And remember, I am with you always, to the end of the age."
MATTHEW 28:18-20

It can be frustrating to live in the "not yet." We're waiting for something we don't know the date of. But here's the cool part: Jesus invites us to join Him on His mission to build a kingdom out of people from every tribe, tongue, and nation. As men, we have a holy mission that's more important than anything else in our lives—more than making money, getting a degree, or winning a title.

It's up to us to make sure our neighbors, our friends, our classmates, and everyone in our lives hears the good news of Jesus.

How does your "holy mission" make you think about what it means to be a man?

Who in your life needs to hear the good news of the gospel?

SEASON 7

PERSONAL BIBLE STUDY

As the disciples preached the resurrected Christ, the Christian faith spread rapidly from Jerusalem. In the Book of Acts we see God using Peter and Paul to declare the gospel and plant churches in cities. After these churches were launched, the apostles wrote letters back to them. The letters, also called epistles, make up the bulk of the New Testament. Often named after the city to which they were written (Galatians to the churches in Galatia, Philippians to the church at Philippi, and so forth), each letter addresses issues in that specific context, and yet, at the same time transcends the context and has deep application for us. There are common themes throughout the letters, and we will look at four of the themes this week: Who Christ is (Day 1), what Christ did (Day 2), who we are (Day 3), and how we should live (Day 4).

CHRIST ABOVE ALL

COLOSSIANS 1:15-20

When you have an hour of free time, what do you wish you were doing? Playing a pick-up game in the driveway? Flopping down in front of the Xbox? Meeting up with your girlfriend at the mall? In other words, what do you hold "supreme" in your life?

Whatever we hold supreme will determine how we live our lives. Maybe you're striving for straight As and a scholarship. Maybe you want to be all-state. In Paul's letter to the Colossians, he made clear who he viewed as supreme—and in doing so set an example for us as men. He wrote, "All things have been created through him and for him … and by him all things hold together" (Col. 1:16-17).

As Christians, we believe that the one God, who created all things, is ultimate. There's nothing more supreme than Him. All our meaning and significance is found in Him. And we believe that Jesus the Christ is God.

In many letters in the New Testament, the apostles devoted time to teaching who Jesus is and to correcting false teaching and beliefs about Him. In the following incredible passage, the apostle Paul reminded his readers and us that Jesus is above all.

Read Colossians 1:15-20.

HE IS THE IMAGE OF THE INVISIBLE GOD

God created us in the image of God, though we are not the image of the invisible God. Jesus is different. He is not created in the image of God because He is the image of God.

Remember the second commandment in the Ten Commandments? One of the reasons God was so adamant to His people not to make any image of Him was because every image we create falls woefully short of the reality of who God is. But Jesus is different. He is not a created image. He does not fall woefully short. He is the image of God.

Think back to our study of the Ten Commandments. How does the second commandment point to Jesus?

THE FIRSTBORN OVER ALL CREATION

The word firstborn, in the original language, refers primarily to position or rank, not chronology. The firstborn son, in this culture, was given authority and rank from the father. The firstborn would receive the inheritance.

Jesus is the firstborn. He is first in rank, position, and authority, and He has received all that is the Father's.

FOR EVERYTHING WAS CREATED BY HIM

Jesus did not come into existence when He was born into this world. He has always existed. He was present in creation. He created the whole world and everything in it. He created the foods we eat, the beaches we enjoy, the sunsets and sunrises we observe. He created Mary, His earthly mother, and He created the trees, which formed the cross He would embrace. He created everything.

IN HEAVEN AND ON EARTH, THE VISIBLE AND THE INVISIBLE, WHETHER THRONES OR DOMINIONS OR RULERS OR AUTHORITIES

The language of "thrones or dominions or ruler or authorities" is used elsewhere in the Scripture, and it describes evil supernatural powers that we do not see. In Ephesians 6:12, Paul wrote that "four struggle is not against flesh and blood, but against the rulers, against the authorities, ... against evil, spiritual forces in the heavens." God created them too. He created all things, even the evil spirits that seek to deceive and destroy.

But understand this: the demons were not created evil; they became evil. They sinned against God and were cast from His presence. In the same way, there are good things that God has created that we distort and ruin in our sinfulness. But this does not change the reality that He has created everything.

What's an example of something good God created that we have distorted and turned sinful?

ALL THINGS HAVE BEEN CREATED THROUGH HIM AND FOR HIM

Not only has Christ created all things, but also all things have been created for Him. All things have been created to bring Him glory. He created the sunset and the sky so we can see visibly the creativity of our invisible God. He created the food we enjoy so when we taste it we might say, "Wow, God is really good to us." He created all things so that all things could bring Him glory. One day even the demons will bow to Him and declare He is God.

HE IS BEFORE ALL THINGS, AND BY HIM ALL THINGS HOLD TOGETHER

You are sitting here in this moment because He is holding the universe together. He is, by His mercy, keeping the sun the exact distance it needs to be from the earth. He is the One keeping the blood flowing through your body. He holds all things together.

HE IS ALSO THE HEAD OF THE BODY, THE CHURCH

He started the church. He is the One who sustains His church. He is the One who keeps us to Himself, who holds on to us despite all our sin and all the junk in our lives. He is the head of the body of Christ.

HE IS THE BEGINNING, THE FIRSTBORN FROM THE DEAD

Just as the firstborn of creation indicates Jesus' rank as the One above all creation and the One who owns all creation—the firstborn from the dead speaks to His supremacy in the resurrection. He is the One who conquered death and has ushered in a new after-death existence for those who follow Him. There is no one greater.

> **What does "firstborn from the dead" mean to you, considering the earlier definition of firstborn as someone with a primary position or rank?**

SO THAT HE MIGHT COME TO HAVE FIRST PLACE IN EVERYTHING

Jesus desires to be first in your life, to have first place over everything in your life. Just as He is the head over all creation, the head over His church, the head over all things, He insists on having first place in your life.

He does not want to be a phase in your life, but rather the ruler over all of your life. He is not content to be something you are into for a season or something you think you will get to later. Christ does not want to be a part of your life, but the King over all of your life.

FOR GOD WAS PLEASED TO HAVE ALL HIS FULLNESS DWELL IN HIM

Because Jesus is fully God, the holiness, righteousness, power, providence, and sovereignty of God dwell fully in Jesus. The love, mercy, compassion, grace, and kindness of God dwell fully in Jesus. And what is absolutely amazing is that when we become Christians, we dwell in Jesus, too.

Go back through this passage and circle or write down all of Paul's "He is" statements about Jesus. Does this make you think differently about Him?

Pray today, thanking God for the gift of Jesus and the sacrifice He made.

NO CONDEMNATION

ROMANS 8:1-4

What does the word "condemned" make you think of? A courtroom? A sentencing? At the heart of it, someone has done something wrong and is being punished.

When we sin, we should expect to be condemned by a holy and perfect God. But Romans 8 has a different message: the awesome news about what Christ has accomplished on our behalf.

As the apostles wrote letters to the churches, they continually reminded the believers what Christ had accomplished in His life, death, and resurrection. Because Christ is the center of the story, the apostles preached Him over and over again. Today, let's look at Romans 8:1-4.

> *Therefore, there is now no condemnation for those in Christ Jesus, because the law of the Spirit of life in Christ Jesus has set you free from the law of sin and death. What the law could not do since it was weakened by the flesh, God did. He condemned sin in the flesh by sending his own Son in the likeness of sinful flesh as a sin offering, in order that the law's requirement would be fulfilled in us who do not walk according to the flesh but according to the Spirit.*
> **ROMANS 8:1-4**

What does this passage mean by "What the law could not do since it was weakened by the flesh"? What could the law not do?

"No condemnation for those in Christ Jesus." Beautiful. To see why, we have to look at condemnation as a legal term: it speaks to both the declaration of guilt and the punishment associated with that guilt. So, for example, if you are caught speeding, your condemnation includes both being declared guilty of going 68 in a 55 MPH zone and receiving the punishment for that offense.

While we deserve condemnation from God because we are sinners, here we see that there now exists *no* condemnation. None. All of God's wrath and condemnation has been replaced with His love and mercy toward you. When God should be angry with us, He is merciful. When He should be condemning, He is forgiving. When you have a bad day or struggle with a particular sin, God is not punishing you. Remember the words above: His wrath, His condemnation, is no more. It has been replaced with His righteousness.

The opposite legal term of condemnation is *justification*. A judge either declares a person to be condemned or declares a person to be justified. There is no condemnation for those of us who are in Christ because Christ justified us. So why is there no condemnation?

Read Romans 8:1-4 again. How would you sum up this passage in one sentence?

There is no condemnation for those of us in Christ because the Holy Spirit grabbed our hearts and changed us, setting us free from "the law of sin and death" (v. 2). The phrase "the law of sin and of death" refers to the general principle that sin has corrupted all of us and that our sin leads to death. We were trapped, imprisoned by sin and death. But the Holy Spirit changed us.

Think back to our earlier lessons about the law. The law God gave His people in the Old Testament was not bad; it was just powerless to change anyone. It can't save us from our sins; it can only point to our need for a Savior. That's why God sent His own Son in the flesh to be a sin offering. This is where the Old Testament story points to the New Testament story: Just as sacrifices in the Old Testament were offered to God so He would be merciful to the people, Christ is our sin offering now. Instead of condemning you, God condemned *sin* in the flesh of Jesus. Your sin was removed from you and placed on Jesus who took your punishment in His flesh. There is no condemnation for you because you don't need it—your sin was already condemned in Christ.

Not a bad deal. But there's more. Because Jesus perfectly obeyed the law, His obedience is given to you in place of your sin. You have fulfilled the law's requirements because Christ's obedience is now yours.

How do we know if we are His? As verse 4 says, those who are His are those who walk with Him, who become more like Him, who walk with the Spirit and don't spend their lives living in the flesh for the things of this world. That's how real men live their lives—and for men like that, there is absolutely no condemnation.

Why did God send Jesus in the New Testament rather than just set new laws? What did Jesus accomplish that the law couldn't?

How would you explain Romans 8:1-4 to someone who's never heard the gospel?

WHO WE ARE

1 PETER 2:9-12

The early Christians knew what it was like to be persecuted. When Rome burned to the ground, some believed the Roman emperor Nero had lit the fire himself. Nero needed someone to blame, so he chose the Christians. When word got out, the persecution escalated. Christians were dispersed throughout "Pontus, Galatia, Cappadocia, Asia, and Bithynia" (1 Pet. 1:1), wondering how to live as disdained people in a world that is not really home. The apostle Peter reminded them who they were, of their great identity as followers of Christ. His words are true of all who belong to Christ.

As you read 1 Peter 2:9-12, highlight every time you see Peter describe who Christians "are."

But you are a chosen race, a royal priesthood, a holy nation, a people for his possession, so that you may proclaim the praises of the one who called you out of darkness into his marvelous light. Once you were not a people, but now you are God's people; you had not received mercy, but now you have received mercy. Dear friends, I urge you as strangers and exiles to abstain from sinful desires that wage war against the soul. Conduct yourselves honorably among the Gentiles, so that when they slander you as evildoers, they will observe your good works and will glorify God on the day he visits.
1 PETER 2:9-12

This passage is incredibly rich.

Chosen Race

Just as God chose Israel in the Old Testament to set His affection upon, God has set His love and affection upon you. You belong to Him because of His promise to you, not because of your goodness. As chosen people, we should rejoice that we belong to Him.

A Royal Priesthood

When God instituted the tabernacle system, only the high priest was allowed to enter the Most Holy Place and be in the presence of God. But now we are royal priests. Christ's death opened a new and living way for us to enter into God's presence anytime, anywhere. As royal priests, we should enjoy His presence.

Why does Christ's death qualify us as a "royal priesthood"?

Holy Nation

God adopted and set Israel apart as His own. As Christians, God has formed us as a new people and declared us to be holy. Because He is holy and has declared us to be holy, we are to live holy lives.

People for His Possession

We no longer belong to ourselves. We are His, which is far better than being slaves to our sin and slaves to ourselves.

Strangers and Temporary Residents

Peter reminded believers that the reason we often feel like we don't fit in this world is because we don't. This world is no longer our home, so we are to abstain from indulging in the sinfulness of this fallen world.

> **How does it make you think differently about your daily life to know that this world is not your home?**

In these verses, Peter used the phrase "so that" twice. Read the passage again and circle both instances.

> *"So that you may proclaim the praises of the one who called you out of darkness into his marvelous light."*
> **1 PETER 2:9**

> *"So that when they slander you as evildoers, they will observe your good works and will glorify God on the day he visits."*
> **1 PETER 2:12**

God gave us a great identity so that we can proclaim His praises to the world. You may not be charged with arson by a Roman emperor—but rest assured your faith will be challenged. How will you respond? How will you be a man in that moment?

We are to live good, faithful, upright lives so that those who do not know God will see us and, by God's grace, be brought to faith in Christ. Then they will join us in glorifying God when He returns.

He is returning. When He does, all that is wrong will be made right. And those who know Him will spend eternity with Him. Until then, we live in a world that is not ours on a mission He has given us. Because of who we are, we are to declare His praises and live honorably among those who do not know Him.

Has anyone ever told you they were proud of you for something you did? How did it make you feel to know they were watching?

What kind of example should you be setting for those who don't know Christ? Think of five words and write them down. Are these words that describe a godly man?

HOW WE SHOULD LIVE

PHILIPPIANS 2:5-11

Have you ever been given a command without a reason why? Maybe you pushed back and were given the classic explanation, "Because I said so." Whether a parent, teacher, coach, or boss, when someone is in authority and refuses to communicate why they want us to do something, our natural inclination is to get mad or frustrated.

The apostles wrote regularly to the early churches, trying to motivate the people to live in God's greatness or grace. It wasn't always easy. So how did they do it? The apostles often rooted the commands God gave in the reality of what Christ has done. In other words, they gave a reason why the church was expected to do something, and that reason was always Jesus.

The apostles' letters are filled with commands, but these commands are always grounded in what Christ has done. That's because if our hearts are not refreshed and renewed with what Christ has done for us, our hearts are unable to obey Him. We need to be in awe of His grace to be motivated to live out the commands.

Let's look at some passages written to the churches. If something is a command, write *command*. If it's referencing what Christ has done, write *Christ*. (The first one is completed as an example.)

Husbands, love your wives __command__ *, just as Christ loved the church and gave Himself for her.* ___Christ___
EPHESIANS 5:25

What should we say then? Should we continue in sin so that grace may multiply? Absolutely not! _____ *How can we who died to sin still live in it?* _____
ROMANS 6:1-2

And be kind and compassionate to one another, forgiving one another _____ *, just as God also forgave you in Christ.* _____
EPHESIANS 4:32

Therefore accept one another _____ *, just as Christ also accepted you,* _____ *, to the glory of God.*
ROMANS 15:7

Now as you excel in everything—in faith, speech, knowledge, and in all diligence, and in your love for us—excel also in this act of grace [giving] _____. For you know the grace of our Lord Jesus Christ: Though he was rich, for your sake he became poor, so that by his poverty you might become rich. _____
2 CORINTHIANS 8:7,9

Do you see the common theme? The commands are there—*Do this*, but they are always rooted in Jesus—*because Christ has done that*. As your heart is constantly refreshed with what Christ has done, you want to obey Him. You want to follow Him. His commands don't feel like a burden because this world is less and less attractive to you as you view Him as greater and greater.

Let's close with this example: *We are to think of others first, because Christ put our salvation ahead of His comfort.*

Do nothing out of selfish ambition or conceit, but in humility consider others as more important than yourselves. Everyone should look out not only for his own interests, but also for the interests of others. Adopt the same attitude as that of Christ Jesus, who, existing in the form of God, did not consider equality with God as something to be exploited. Instead he emptied himself by assuming the form of a servant, taking on the likeness of humanity. And when he had come as a man, he humbled himself by becoming obedient to the point of death—even to death on a cross. For this reason God highly exalted him and gave him the name that is above every name, so that at the name of Jesus every knee will bow—in heaven and on earth and under the earth—and every tongue will confess that Jesus Christ is Lord, to the glory of God the Father.
PHILIPPIANS 2:3-11

How does Christ's sacrifice motivate you to live your life?

If someone asked you to tell them in a couple sentences why Jesus had to die on the cross, what would you say?

Pray today, thanking Him for His sacrifice, as well as the commands we were left to follow in faith.

8

SEASON 8

A BETTER BEGINNING

WHAT WILL BE IS EVEN BETTER

	2000 BC	1400 BC	1000 BC	600 BC	AD	AD 30	
CREATION & FALL	**PROMISE & A PEOPLE**	**RESCUE & LAW**	**LAND & KINGDOM**	**EXILE & RETURN**	**JESUS**	**A NEW PEOPLE**	**A BETTER BEGINNING**

Revelation marks the end of the Bible story, but really it's just a better beginning of the story. Think back to the world God created in Genesis, how everything was perfect, and we were living in unity with Him. After sin entered the world, everything was ruined—but Jesus' return fixes this broken place and makes everything right. The pain of this world will pale in comparison to the glory that's going to be revealed within us.

Read Revelation 5:1–10 out loud.

The Lamb is the only one worthy to open the scroll. How is the Lamb described in verse 6? It looks like it has been *slaughtered*. Jesus' blood is what makes Him worthy.

> **Look at verse 10: It says all the people "from every tribe and language and people and nation" will reign on the earth. Does that include us? What does that mean?**

Heaven isn't a place in the clouds where we go to play a harp and fly around. Revelation describes it as a "new earth," where God dwells with humanity:

> *Then I saw a new heaven and a new earth; for the first heaven and the first earth had passed away, and the sea no more. I also saw the holy city, the new Jerusalem, coming down out of heaven from God, prepared like a bride adorned for her husband. Then I heard a loud voice from the throne: Look, God's dwelling is with humanity, and he will live with them. They will be his peoples, and God himself will be with them and will be their God. He will wipe away every tear from their eyes. Death will be no more; grief, crying, and pain will be no more, because the previous things have passed away … I did not see a temple in it, because the Lord God the Almighty and the Lamb are its temple.*
> **REVELATION 21:1-4,22**

Death is gone. Grief, crying, pain—over. We look forward to heaven because Jesus is there, the One who rescued us, and that means we have a new earth where all the negative impacts of sin are ended because of His sacrifice. There is no sanctuary, the verse says, because the Lamb is the sanctuary. What an amazing image.

> *Then he showed me the river of the water of life, clear as crystal, flowing from the throne of God and of the Lamb down the middle of the city's main street. The tree of life was on each side of the river, bearing twelve kinds of fruit, producing its fruit every month. The leaves of the tree are for healing the nations, and there will no longer be any curse. The throne of God and of the Lamb will be in the city, and his servants will worship him.*
> **REVELATION 22:1-3**

Remember the tree of life? Think back to Season 1—when Adam and Eve disobeyed God, sin entered the world. God blocked the way to the tree of life. But here, sin is done away with because of Jesus, and there is access once again to the tree of life. Sin is gone. Grief is gone. The tree of life is for healing the nations, and there is no longer a curse. This is the better beginning.

Here are four things we see in this passage:

1. THE NATIONS ARE GATHERED

There are people in heaven from every tribe, tongue, and nation. This is why God gave us the command He did last season to bring all the people to Him—because that's what heaven looks like.

> **Do you ever get uncomfortable being around people who are different than you? When you picture "all tribes" gathered in heaven, what do you imagine?**

2. THE CURSE IS REVERSED

When sin entered the world, everything was cursed. In one move, suddenly we had death. We had illness. We had war. We had cancer. We had divorce. We had famines, earthquakes, and plagues. These are the effects of living in a sinful world. But when Christ returns, He makes everything new. There's no more curse.

> **Some definitions of curse use the word "afflicted." If we are afflicted with a curse, then what's the word to describe what Jesus did?**

3. EVIL IS DESTROYED

Heaven isn't just a place where goodness reigns—it's a place where evil is destroyed. Because sin violates God's character, it must be punished. We can live without the burden of our own sin forever and ever, because of Jesus.

Why must evil be destroyed for the kingdom of God to reign?

4. CHRIST IS ENJOYED

Heaven is a good and perfect place where all is restored. But the centerpiece of heaven is not the people we've lost here. It's Jesus. He is who we long to see and who quenches our souls.

Heaven isn't for guys who just don't want to go to hell. Heaven is for those of us who have been rescued by Jesus and long to worship Him with our entire lives. That's what it means to be a man: to long for Him. To want Jesus. To make Him the centerpiece of your life.

All of the Bible is about Jesus. That's the larger story we've been seeing. Jesus Christ is the center of the Bible, He's the center of heaven, and He longs to be the center of your life.

When you picture heaven, what do you see?

How would you explain to someone how the idea of heaven is rooted in the Old Testament?

How does this picture of heaven make you think about what it means to be a man?

LEADER
GUIDE

SESSION ONE

Prepare

- Begin this first week with an activity to break the ice and get your guys interacting. You'll want them to speak up during your sessions, so do your best to create an open, comfortable, and (most importantly) confidential space.

- Open by playing "Where Do You Stand?" Draw an imaginary line down the room: On one end is one extreme, and on the other is another extreme. Ask the group several opinion-based questions. To answer, everyone will choose somewhere to stand along the imaginary line according to how strong their opinion is. For example, if you ask students "football or baseball?" they will stand on the far left if they strongly prefer football, and on the far right-hand side if they strongly prefer baseball. If they are neutral, they will stand in the middle. Have fun coming up with your own questions. A few to get you started: Rock or country? Cake or pie? Winter or summer? Prom or homecoming?

Engage

- Since this study is specifically about manhood, set the tone for your group by being confident, honest, and appropriately vulnerable. Let them know that this is their chance to get real. Use their names, look them in the eye, and don't let them be content to sit in silence. As you get to know your group, you'll get more confident in how to engage them. Maybe it's with food or a quick game of pick-up basketball beforehand. Meet them where they are.

- This week is about who God is, who we are, and how we messed that up. Many guys will have heard the creation story many times. Emphasize how it isn't just a story of where the world began, but where the gospel began. Show them how everything points to Jesus.

- This first session is an important chance to shatter some of the assumptions about what it means to be a man. Go around the group and ask what some of these assumptions are (you can't be emotional, you have to be strong, you can't be vulnerable, etc.), and counter those with images of Jesus.

Before You Go

- Remind guys to do the personal study days on their own. Consider pairing them up into accountability partners to check on each other during the week, or send them encouraging texts yourself.

- Close by praying for your group. Pray specifically over the guys and for meaningful time together that will help grow their faith.

SESSION TWO

Prepare

- Start by asking the group how their personal study days went. Where and when did they do their sessions? Did they find a system that works for them? Did they learn anything surprising? As you talk it out as a group, guys will be encouraged to keep going and do the work on their own.

- Ask the group to name some of the men they look up to, or who set good examples of manhood. It could be people in their lives or famous coaches or celebrities. This will give you a good baseline for what your guys think about manhood and the types of influence speaking into their lives. Challenge them to say specifically why they look up to these men.

Engage

- To a teenage guy, sometimes the Old Testament can feel like learning a history lesson. Remember the point isn't to memorize a Sunday school lesson, but to point your group to Jesus. Show them where He enters these stories and how all of the Bible—even the stories that are harder to get through—points to Him.

- The story of Abraham and Isaac is about the ultimate sacrifice—the same sacrifice Jesus would make for us. Find another contemporary example of men who made a major sacrifice, like the soldiers on D-Day. Start a conversation about what it says about manhood to be willing to make a sacrifice, and how that points to Jesus.

- Abraham's story is also a good opportunity to open a conversation about father-son relationships and how your group has been impacted by their dads, but be sensitive to the fact that some may not want to share or may not have good relationships with their fathers.

Before You Go

- Remind the group to do their personal study days this week. Send them encouraging texts or find small, non-intrusive ways to check in throughout the week, like a group email.

- Close by praying for your group. Pray specifically that this lesson would point guys to Jesus and make real for them the sacrifice that He made for us.

SESSION THREE

Prepare

- The story of Moses is a good chance to talk about leadership. Start by handing out pens and paper to everyone in the group and tell them to write down some of the characteristics of a good leader. Everyone should write down at least three.

- Invite students to read them aloud or write them on a whiteboard or flip board. Then compare them to Moses—you'll probably find that many of the things we consider essential to good leaders (confidence, education, a good upbringing, boldness) weren't a part of Moses character at all. God chose to use him—and He can use us, too.

- A lesson on leadership is also a good chance to pull from some contemporary examples. Bring recent news stories of politicians, athletes, celebrities, or other people who showed good—and bad—examples of leadership, and discuss why their examples are either good or not.

Engage

- The story of the Israelites is a beautiful example of how God keeps His promises. It can be difficult for teenage guys to remember that sometimes in the busyness and frustration of daily life, but use this story to remind them that God has promised to be with them and always will be.

- After their deliverance, God commanded the Israelites to "not have other gods" besides Him. We fill our lives with little gods, things that distract us from Him and lead us away from Jesus. Talk about this with your guys—school, girls, work, sports. These things are good, but they can also be distractions.

Before You Go

- Remind the group to do their personal study days this week and check in with them as you go.

- Close by praying for your group. Pray specifically that God would reveal to them what makes a leader and prepare them for the times in their lives they will have to lead. Thank Him for keeping His promises to be with us and for delivering us time and time again, even when we didn't deserve it.

SESSION FOUR

Prepare

- Start by asking guys how their personal study days went. Don't be surprised if they've fallen off a bit—four weeks in, they're going to need some encouragement to keep going. Stress that this week's lesson is about discipline, and that part of being a man is being disciplined. These personal study days aren't homework— they're a chance to shape them into godly men. Are they willing to do that?

Engage

- Discipline can be a hard trait for us to handle with God, especially when we talk about His love for us. But it's because of that love that He disciplines us. Ask guys about the authority figures in their lives—their coaches, dads, teachers, band directors, and bosses. Are they strict? Why? If it's someone who cares about them, then it's because they want the best for them and set a high standard.

- Hammer home these verses from Hebrews: "Endure suffering as discipline: God is dealing with you as sons. For what son is there that a father does not discipline? But if you are without discipline—which all receive—then you are illegitimate children and not sons" (Heb. 12:7-8).

- Think back to the list of "other gods" you came up with last week—the things that get in the way of us worshiping Him alone. God knows we won't be satisfied until we only worship Him. That's why He disciplines us. So what are some practical things you can do to prioritize these things less, and Him more? Maybe it's less time practicing and more time in the Word. Maybe it's choosing church over your girlfriend. Talk it out as a group.

Before You Go

- This week is the halfway point, and some of your guys might be tempted to slack off. Don't let them. Reinforce the importance of personal study and check in with them through a quick group text or email blast this week.

- Close by praying for your group. Thank God for His discipline, because it shows He loves us and thinks of us as sons. Pray that your guys would take God's discipline as a blessing and work to worship Him alone in their lives.

SESSION FIVE

Prepare

- This is the last lesson of the Old Testament before we see Jesus enter the scene. Revisit the first four weeks before you start—remind them what each lesson was about, then ask the group how each one points to Jesus.

- This lesson discusses how God keeps His promises to His people. Ask guys to think back to something they promised—maybe it was to their parents, or a teammate, or a girlfriend. The words "I promise" are heavy. They're a covenant. Did they keep that promise? Have they ever felt the ramifications of breaking a promise?

Engage

- Each week, we see God's people turn away from Him, despite His provision and promises. While we aren't building literal idols today, we are serving lots of them. Remind your group that this behavior is why Jesus had to come: because He alone was the ultimate fulfillment of God's promises—then and now. When we worship something other than Him, we take away from His sacrifice for us.

- Rather than talk at the group during your time together, let them talk amongst themselves in pairs or groups of three. Give them this verse from Ezekiel: *But I will remember the covenant I made with you in the days of your youth, and I will establish a permanent covenant with you* (Ezek. 16:60). What covenant does this verse refer to? What covenant has God made with us today? How is Jesus the fulfillment of that promise? Float around from group to group and listen to the conversations, encouraging them as you go.

Before You Go

- Remind your group that next week, Jesus enters the scene. Jesus, the fulfillment of everything we've read. Jesus, the Lamb of God that Scripture has been pointing to since the garden of Eden. Tell them that it's extra important they do their personal study pages this week so they can fully understand why Jesus had to come.

- Pray for your group, thanking God for His covenant with them and for your time together. Ask Him to protect the time you share together and to teach guys about the things He has promised them. Ask God to help keep your guys strong and committed this week as they live in that promise.

SESSION SIX

Prepare

- Now that Jesus is on the scene, you'll be dealing with Bible stories that your group is probably more familiar with and more comfortable discussing. Bring them to life and really engage your group—this is everything we've been leading up to!

- Jesus is the ultimate model of manhood. On a whiteboard, flip board, or just a piece of paper, make two lists as a group: What the world says a man is like, and what Jesus was like. Have the group call out words that come to mind. Your first list will include things like tough, brave, unemotional, disciplined, and hard-working, while your second should include things like loving, devoted, friend to sinners, and humble. That's the guide to manhood—not the world.

Engage

- This is an important week to really bring the study together for your group. Jesus is where the Bible story kicks into high gear, but it's also a continuation of the Old Testament. Jesus is here because of what God promised His people, and because they were longing for a king.

- What do we look for in a leader? Look at your list of traits of Jesus. Are those the words they would use to describe the men of authority in their lives? Why, or why not?

- Use this lesson as a chance to present the gospel, and invite anyone in your group who is not a Christian to ask Jesus into their lives. His death is for them, and their willingness to give their hearts to Him is the manliest thing they could ever do. Offer to talk to anyone privately, even over text later if they want. Be there for them anytime they need you.

Before You Go

- Now that we just have a couple weeks left, remind guys of the importance of finishing strong. Jesus did it, and so should we. The personal study pages this week will paint a full picture of the miracle of His coming to earth, and it's critical that they read them.

- As you pray over your group, thank God for Jesus and for coming to earth as a fulfillment of God's promises to us. Thank Him for keeping His promises, always.

SESSION SEVEN

Prepare

- Spend some time going over the stories from last week's personal study pages. These are stories guys may have already known. But how did they think about them in terms of what it means to be a man? What kind of picture of manhood does Jesus give us? Recap each story briefly and try to kick off your session with some group discussion.

Engage

- As we wind toward the end of our time together, this week's lesson focuses on the "so what" that comes after the beauty of Christ's story. Why is it so important that all of Scripture points to Him? Because of the "already/not yet" nature of God's kingdom: His kingdom has already begun, but it's not yet fulfilled. That's why we have the Holy Spirit.

- Go around the group and ask guys to give examples of things they are waiting on or looking forward to. It could be graduation, getting a license, going to prom, leaving for college, or Friday night's game. Is it difficult for them to wait? Why is God making us wait for the fulfillment of His kingdom?

- Spend some quality time with the discussion questions, particularly as they relate to the Holy Spirit. Your group may have a hard time articulating what it is, or how they would describe it. That's OK. Use this as a safe space to let them ask questions, even if it's difficult to articulate the answers.

Before You Go

- This is the last week for personal study pages, so implore them to finish strong. Being a man is about finishing what you started. Now is not the time to quit. Encourage them throughout the week with texts or email blasts, and consider doing something fun or bringing food to your last meeting next week.

- Pray over your group, thanking God for the Holy Spirit and asking Him to reveal Himself to your guys this week. Thank Him for the model of manhood that we get from Jesus and ask for His help as we strive to be better men this week.

SESSION EIGHT

Prepare

- This is the last week together, so start by asking each guy to share one thing he's taken from this study, or one thing he's learned about what it means to be a man of God. Start by sharing your own, and don't be afraid to go deeper and use their answers as launching points for group discussion.

- This week is about heaven and the coming kingdom of God, so it could be fun to start with some of their preconceived notions of what heaven is. What do they think about when they think about heaven? Clouds? Angels? Harps? Revelation has a lot more to say than that.

Engage

- This last lesson is a chance to go back to the beginning and recap how everything in the Bible follows one story arc, leading here. Go back to the story of Adam and Eve and the tree of life. We start in the garden with God, and that's where we end—in His presence, with sin banished and His righteousness restored.

- It can be difficult to live for heaven when we're so busy, especially when you're a teenager and you're worried about school, sports, work, college, and girls. But being a man means living for more than what's on this earth. Remind your group that Jesus' story didn't end with his death, and neither does ours—because of His resurrection, we have so much more to live for. That starts now.

- Pass out some paper and pens and ask each guy to write down one commitment they are going to make going forward. It might be about how they want to grow as a man. It might be about strengthening their faith. What are they going to do differently? They don't have to share, but if someone wants to, great. Use it as a deep discussion about how knowing the story of the Bible changes you.

Before You Go

- See if someone will lead the group in your final prayer, or offer multiple people the chance to speak up. Thank God for the things He has revealed to you, and thank Him for the chance to keep growing.

- Remind your guys before they go that the conversation doesn't end here—Jesus wants to be the centerpiece of their lives. If they have any questions, they can come to you, their parents, or their youth pastor. Check in with them via text or email, or consider having a low-key discipleship gathering in a few weeks for ice cream or pizza. Be a strong, consistent advocate for godly manhood in their lives.

ENDNOTES

[1] Robert Haldane. *Commentary on Romans.* (Titus Books, 2013), e-book.

[2] LifeWay Research and Ligonier Ministries. *The State of American Theology: Knowing the Truth, Loving the Church, Reaching our Neighbors.* (Nashville, Tenn.: LifeWay Research, 2014), 4. Available from Internet: https://www.gospelproject.com/ebook-download/

[3] John R.W. Stott. *The Cross of Christ.* (InterVarsity Press: Downer's Grove, Ill., 2006). 194.

[4] Michael Jordan. "Forbes Quotes," *Forbes* [online]. Accessed 1 October 2017. Available from the Internet: https://www.forbes.com/quotes/11194/.

[5] Charles H. Spurgeon. *Treasury of David.* Online. Accessed 25 October 2016. Available from Internet: www.spurgeon.org/treasury.

[6] Martin Luther, translated by Bruce A. Cameron. *Reading the Psalms with Luther: The Psalter for Individual and Family Devotions.* (Concordia Publishing House, 2007). ebook.

[7] Adam Aspinall. "Stonehenge archaeologists have been digging in the wrong place—for 90 YEARS." *The Mirror.* 21 November 2013. Accessed 25 October 2016. Available from Internet: http://www.mirror.co.uk/news/uk-news/stonehenge-archaeologists-been-digging-wrong-2813818.

Quote on back cover:

Edmund Clowney. *The Unfolding Mystery, Second Edition: Discovering Christ in the Old Testament.* (Phillipsburg, New Jersey: P & R Publishing, 2013), 12.

RECOMMENDED
READING AND SOURCES

The following books were extremely valuable and helpful during preparation for this Bible study. I read through them multiple times, and the authors helped form my thoughts and presentation probably more than I realize.

- *The Drama of Scripture* by Craig Bartholomew and Michael Goheen

- *God's Big Picture* by Vaughn Roberts

- *Telling God's Story* by Preben Vang and Terry Carter

- *According to Plan* by Graeme Goldsworthy

- *The God Who Is There* by D. A. Carson

- *Living God's Word* by J. Scott Duvall & J. Daniel Hays

- *From Creation to New Creation* by Tim Chester

- *A Walk Through the Bible* by Lesslie Newbigin

- *The Scarlet Thread Through the Scriptures* by W.A. Criswell

- *Seamless* by Angie Smith

- *The Cross of Christ* by John Stott

Additionally, the timeline I use throughout the study and the map of the Northern and Southern kingdom in Season 5 are adapted from the Biblical Illustrator team at LifeWay Christian Resources. The chart labeled "Cycle of Sin" in Season 4 is adapted from the chart provided by J. Scott Duvall and J. Daniel Hays in *Living God's Word*.

DIVIDED KINGDOM

MEDITERRANEAN
SEA

ISRAEL

★
Samaria

•Bethel

★
Jerusalem

JUDAH

DEAD
SEA

Dan

Lake
Huleh

Sea of
Galilee

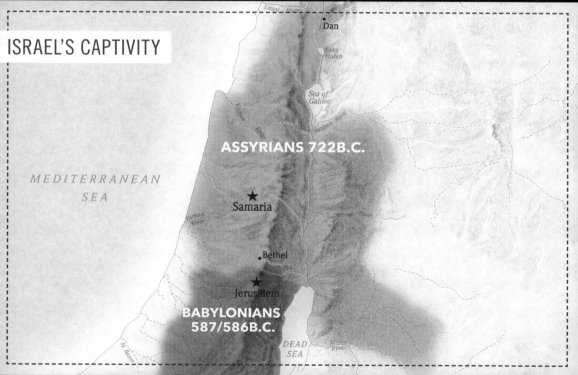

ISRAEL'S CAPTIVITY

MEDITERRANEAN
SEA

ASSYRIANS 722B.C.

★
Samaria

•Bethel

★
Jerusalem

BABYLONIANS
587/586B.C.

DEAD
SEA

Dan

Lake
Huleh

Sea of
Galilee

THE STORY
OF GOD

CREATION AND FALL
The self-sufficient and eternal God lovingly creates a perfect creation with humanity as His crowning work. Falling for Satan's temptation, humanity rebels and sin enters the world bringing death, pain, and strife. Instead of giving up on humanity, God promises that from the womb of a woman will come the One who will crush Satan's head.

PROMISE AND A PEOPLE
God pursues Abraham, a man from an idol-worshiping family who has no children with his wife, and promises that he will be the father of many nations. God promises land to Abraham and assures him that all nations will be blessed through his offspring. God continues to be faithful to this family. He restates the promise to Abraham's son Isaac and grandson Jacob (who is renamed Israel). A famine strikes the promised land, so Jacob and the family move to Egypt where one of Jacob's sons, Joseph, is already there to provide for the family.

RESCUE AND LAW
The family becomes a nation while living in Egypt, but also becomes enslaved to the Egyptians. God raises up Moses to lead His people to freedom. During a tenth plague, God strikes dead the firstborn son of everyone living in Egypt, but "passes over" Israel as they put the blood of lambs on their doorposts. After miraculously rescuing His people, God gives His people the law. He also instructs them to build a tabernacle and offer sacrifices so He may dwell among them.

LAND AND KINGDOM
God brings His people, through their leader Joshua, into the promised land. When God's people worship the gods of the nations surrounding them, God disciplines them through the attacks of surrounding nations. God raises up judges (or rulers) to rescue His people and call them to repentance. They beg for a king to be like other nations, and God gives them Saul. God raises up a new king, David, and promises that his kingdom will never end. The family that turned into a nation is now a kingdom. David's son, Solomon, builds a temple to replace the tabernacle.

EXILE AND RETURN

Solomon takes foreign wives and allows their foreign gods to clutter the land. His son continues the line of rulers and the kingdom is divided into the Northern Kingdom (Israel) and the Southern Kingdom (Judah). Prophets confront the people but they persist in their idolatry. The Northern Kingdom falls to Assyria and the Southern Kingdom is carried away into Babylonian captivity. When they are freed, they return to a nation and kingdom far less glorious than before and are still unable to keep their promises.

JESUS

A descendant of Adam, Abraham, and David, Jesus is the One who crushes the head of Satan, will bless all nations, and reigns forever. Jesus, the God-Man, enters humanity through the womb of a virgin, perfectly obeys the law that we could never obey, dies as the once-and-for-all sacrifice for our sins, and rises from the dead, conquering Satan, sin, and death. He inaugurates His eternal kingdom and secures salvation for His people.

A NEW PEOPLE

After His ascension to heaven, Jesus sends the promised Holy Spirit and His disciples turn the world upside down preaching the good news of Jesus. In the midst of intense persecution, the gospel spreads, and Gentiles and Jews form a new people. Churches are planted in cities, and apostles write letters encouraging and instructing the people in the grace of Christ and their response to His grace.

A BETTER BEGINNING

A time is coming where God's people—people from every tribe, tongue, and nation who have been rescued by Christ—will enjoy Him and His rule forever in perfect harmony. Satan will be crushed, the effects of sin will be reversed, and all things will be made new.

THE STORY OF GOD
TIMELINE

2000 BC **1400 BC** **1000 BC**

| CREATION & FALL | PROMISE & A PEOPLE | RESCUE & LAW | LAND & KINGDOM |

The self-sufficient and eternal God lovingly creates a perfect creation with humanity as His crowning work. Falling for Satan's temptation, humanity rebels and sin enters the world bringing death, pain, and strife. Instead of giving up on humanity, God promises that from the womb of a woman will come the One who will crush Satan's head.

God pursues Abraham, a man from an idol worshiping family who has no children with his wife, and promises that he will be the father of many nations. God promises land to Abraham and assures him that all nations will be blessed through his offspring. God continues to be faithful to this family. He restates the promise to Abraham's son Isaac and grandson Jacob (who is renamed Israel). A famine strikes the promised land, so Jacob and the family move to Egypt where one of Jacob's sons, Joseph, is already there to provide for the family.

The family becomes a nation while living in Egypt, but also becomes enslaved to the Egyptians. God raises up Moses to lead His people to freedom. During a tenth plague, God strikes dead the first born son of everyone living in Egypt, but "passes over" Israel as they put the blood of lambs on their doorposts. After miraculously rescuing His people, God gives His people the law. He also instructs them to build a tabernacle and offer sacrifices so He may dwell among them.

God brings His people, through their leader Joshua, into the promised land. When God's people worship the gods of the nations surrounding them, God disciplines them through the attacks of surrounding nations. God raises up judges (or rulers) to rescue His people and call them to repentance. The people beg for a king to be like other nations, and God gives them Saul. God raises up a new king, David, and promises that his kingdom will never end. The family that turned into a nation is now a kingdom. David's son, Solomon, builds a temple to replace the tabernacle.

600 BC	**AD**	**AD 30**	
	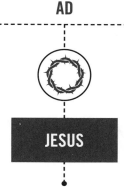		
EXILE & RETURN	**JESUS**	**A NEW PEOPLE**	**A BETTER BEGINNING**

Solomon takes foreign wives and allows their foreign gods to clutter the land. His son continues the line of rulers and the kingdom is divided into the Northern Kingdom (Israel) and the Southern Kingdom (Judah). Prophets confront the people but they persist in their idolatry. The Northern Kingdom falls to Assyria and the Southern Kingdom is carried away into Babylonian captivity. When they are freed, they return to a nation and kingdom far less glorious than before and are still unable to keep their promises.

A descendant of Adam, Abraham, and David, Jesus is the One who crushes the head of Satan, will bless all nations, and reigns forever. Jesus, the God-Man, enters humanity through the womb of a virgin, perfectly obeys the law that we could never obey, dies as the once-and-for-all sacrifice for our sins, and rises from the dead, conquering Satan, sin, and death. He inaugurates His eternal kingdom and secures salvation for His people.

After His ascension to heaven, Jesus sends the promised Holy Spirit and His disciples turn the world upside down preaching the good news of Jesus. In the midst of intense persecution, the gospel spreads, and Gentiles and Jews form a new people. Churches are planted in cities, and apostles write letters encouraging and instructing the people in the grace of Christ and their response to His grace.

A time is coming where God's people—people from every tribe, tongue, and nation who have been rescued by Christ—will enjoy Him and His rule forever in perfect harmony. Satan will be crushed, the effects of sin will be reversed, and all things will be made new.